I could tell you I don't give a damn what people think about my books but to be honest, I do care what these fine folks think:

Book One
Chew With Your Mind Open, Liftoff and Ascent

"The best book on how to work in advertising that I've ever come across."
Toby Barlow, CCO, Lafayette American

"Not only one of the most genuinely useful advertising guides I've read but one of the warmest and most entertaining to read – a rare combination."
Andrew Boulton, Head of Copy + Author of *Copywriting Is*

"Cameron Day is advertising royalty, being the son of Guy Day, co-founder of the legendary creative agency, Chiat/Day. But far from acting royal, Cameron shares his struggles to make it on his own - warts, gaffes, kerfuffles and all. I've never been great at math, but I give this book a 6-star rating out of 5."
Howie Cohen, Author of *I Can't Believe I Lived The Whole Thing*

"For someone just starting out in the industry, there were so many useful lessons to learn and it's told in such a genuine way."
Sabrina Cavanagh, Art Director at Vail Resorts, Boulder, CO

"Cameron's superpower is his knack for teaching, training and mentoring young people. An awesome read!"
Jeff Graham, President and CMO at Cactus, Denver, CO

"Not your standard blow-sunshine-up-your-ass, feel-good platitudes about creativity. This book should be up there right on the shelf with Luke Sullivan's seminal *Whipple, Squeeze This* and Thomas Kemeny's *Junior.*"
Kenneth L. Marcus, ACD + VCU Brand Center Adjunct Professor

"Whether just starting out, or a veteran, you'll enjoy every grimacing detail of advertising's hilarious pitfalls and prideful rewards. Like working in advertising itself, Cameron's recounts are joyful, painful, and insightful. But never boring."
Will Chau, Vice President of Creative and Design at Whole Foods Market

"This is a business book wrapped in bacon. All the myths of advertising rolled up into one book of truths. Add the hard-hitting professional advice, and you have yourself one fine chew."
Bryan Carter, CEO of Think Creative Intelligence

"I wish I'd had this book decades ago. How to deal with people, how to show up with integrity, how to trust the process. It's a joy to read."
Shayna Levin Brown, Founder at Chez Boom Audio

"Truth told with humor and masterful, natural wit, with lessons for everyone. *Chew With Your Mind Open* is a great look under the tent of advertising. No one paints this world as well as Cameron Day."
Rick Russo, President, CCO at Arnold Worldwide

Book Two
Spittin' Chiclets, The Messy Middle Years

"This is Cam's second book. I think it is even better than the first. And it's one of the few books that offer advice on how to be a better creative director."
Luke Sullivan, Author of *Hey, Whipple, Squeeze This: The Classic Guide to Creating Great Ads*

"Nobody has written a better book about how to survive and thrive in the middle of your career than Cameron Day."
Mark Jenson, Senior Lecturer at the U of MN Hubbard School of Journalism and Mass Communication, Advertising and Brand Consultant

"Required reading for anyone trying to resurrect their career. It's like having a caring older brother extending a hand to pull you out of the quicksand of career missteps - or if you're lucky enough - point them out ahead of time."
Jolly Heath, Art Director

"Cameron Day gives us an entertaining and insightful look into the world of big-time advertising. His clever observations and brilliant storytelling leave you wanting more."
Terry Balagia, Novelist, Published Author and Educator

"There's a lot of advice out there. Most of it is bullshit. from people who are good at bullshit. Cameron Day is the opposite. He's seen it all with a unique POV that very few can offer. He's also a gifted writer able to deliver insights anyone at any level can appreciate. Highly recommended."
Joe Alexander, Former CCO of The Martin Agency, Freelance Copywriter and Creative Director

"This book is a fantastic way to learn some award-winning mistakes to avoid in the middle of your career."
Ben Levy, Creative Director, Presentation Coach

"Truth be told, your current skills may not transfer naturally to becoming a creative director. So do it the unnatural way – read *Spittin' Chiclets*. Both sacred and profane, every page is jammed with thoughtful and irreverent wisdom that can totally save your corner office-seeking ass."
Chuck Guest, Owner of Prime Chuck Creative

"If you're in your "Messy Middle Years" like I am, you've learned what a bloodbath the ad industry can be. But within these pages, you'll find Day arming you with everything necessary to fend off hockey sticks, fists, arrows, spears -- and anything else the ad biz may throw at you."
Lesly Pyle, ACD/Copywriter, Author

"Day's stories and pointers are grounded in real, human terms. *Spittin' Chiclets* is a North Star for ad creatives to follow."
Howard Ibach, Creative Brief Expert, Online Instructor, Author, and co-host of *The Brief Brother's* podcast

"This is by far the best, most brutally honest book on what it's like to work in the advertising world. Buy this book now."
Ryan Gray, Chief Creative Officer, Co-founder, Beckert

"Cameron Day is the guy who's done it all and thankfully, has written about his experiences along the way. His book is inspirational, educational, and entertaining all at once."
Vikki Ross, Copywriter, Brand and TOV Consultant

Book Three
Stones & Sticks,
The Highest Altitudes of Your
Ad Career

"*Stones & Sticks* is like settling down in an overstuffed leather chair in a club where good whiskey is served in crystal glasses. You get an insider look at the advertising business impossible to find elsewhere. And to complete your education grab the first two books in this must-have trilogy *Chew With Your Mind Open* and *Spittin' Chiclets*. But don't lend them to your friends in the ad world. You'll probably never see 'em again. The books, not your friends."
Scott Frothingham, Wordwrangler, Carrotdangler, Storyteller, Goal-oriented writing

"A surprisingly hilarious manual for surviving the cutthroat business of advertising, Day's gonzo style is a must-read for those crazy enough to dive into the ad world. It makes *Mad Men* look like child's play."
Tay Guan Hin, CCO, BBDO/Singapore

"Ever looked at an ad and wondered about the gallons of blood, sweat and tears that went into that 30 seconds? Well. Come on in, the water's lovely within the pages of Cameron's new book, *Stones & Sticks*. Between the covers, Cameron shares his decades of experience with panache, verve and charisma. This book is a refresher course in realness, with Cameron sharing truths in his inimitable way on topics as diverse as dealing with the audacity of those who declare themselves biologically funny and Concept Karens, to what you need to understand about yourself in order to be a good freelancer, to the perils of having a client who thinks they're smarter than their customer. This book is a treasure trove of crackers, with every page sparkling with actionable advice for creatives at every level. My personal favourite? "Don't try to write like me. Write like you." While that's technically a Jean Craig special, Cameron is canny enough to attribute it - he could have borrowed it, blown his own trumpet, but that wouldn't be very *Stones & Sticks*. All in all, this book is a long cool drink at the end of a hard day. Come for the Storytimes, stay for the wild ride."
Sarah Coffey, Senior Writer, The Tenth Man, Dublin, Ireland

"Iconic stories, hard-won wisdom, and important lessons for all. A masterclass and a fun romp."
Jen Costello, Chief Strategy Officer, TBWA\Chiat\Day

"A wealth of insight, intrigue, and wit. I'm a better account person after reading Day's third installment."
Lisa Tanner, Executive Director, Client Engagement, VMLY&R

"I'm squarely in the middle of my advertising career. Smack dab, 12 years in. I'm glad to have the hard-earned wisdom from this hilarious, practical, and generous book sooner rather than later."
Eddie Shleyner, founder & author of VeryGoodCopy.com

"This book isn't for the faint-hearted. It's for the big-hearted, strong enough to put a load of love into their advertising career."
Vikki Ross, Copywriter, Brand and TOV Consultant

"If you want to stay alive in this business, use every word Cameron writes to sharpen your own pen. Then in need, use that pen as a machete. I promise you you'll come out of the ad jungle richer than ever."
Simone Nobili, Author of *Transatlantic*, a video podcast with a lot of water in it

All books in the Advertising Survival Guide trilogy are available through Amazon Books in print and Kindle editions, or hand-signed by the author at www.iamcameronday.com

Graphic design: Andrew Mark Lawrence
Cover concept: Beau Hanson
Cover photography: The Voorhes
Archival Artwork: CSA Images
Sticky Intellect logo: Robert Lin

Published by Sticky Intellect, 2021
Text: © 2021, Cameron Day
Foreword: © 2020, Lee Clow

STICKY INTELLECT
PUBLISHING

The Advertising Survival Guide
Stage One: Launch and Ascent

CHEW WITH YOUR MIND OPEN

by **Cameron Day** with foreword by Lee Clow

CONTENTS

FOREWORD

Hello. Let me introduce myself, I'm Lee Clow. I've been making advertising for 50 years. So I know a few things about the subject of this book. But Cameron Day is a writer. I'm an art director. Cameron has worked at a lot of different ad agencies. I've spent 50 years at one. So why am I writing this FOREWORD? Well, the advertising agency I spent my entire career at is Chiat/Day. The Chiat is Jay Chiat, and the Day is Guy Day, Cameron's father.

That's Guy on the right. And his influence on my career and Cameron's life is a special thing we have in common. This book is full of agency stories, people stories, insights, observations, and fun from Cameron's adventures in the advertising business. And you'll learn a lot from his experiences and lessons learned. But many times in this book you'll feel the wisdom of Guy Day, who taught us both the importance of being passionate, believing in yourself, and most importantly integrity.

So while all the, as Cameron puts it, food for thought you'll discover in CHEW WITH YOUR MIND OPEN comes from Cameron's journey from agency to agency, client to client, I'd like to think that you'll also feel the guiding spirit of one of the most important creative thinkers and inspirational leaders in the history of the advertising business. Mr. Day Sr.

Lee Clow,
Global Director, Media Arts, TBWA/Chiat/Day

INTRODUCTION

You may wonder what I was thinking when I wrote the Advertising Survival Guide. I know my friends and family did when I put these thoughts in writing over a couple of years time between freelance assignments.

I was thinking, first and foremost, about how much fun it is to solve problems for a living and about how few businesses continue to confound its practitioners the way modern brand-building does.

I was thinking about just how fortunate I've been to have met so many smart people who knew so much more than I did.

I was thinking about what I'd tell anyone interested in having a long and rewarding career in advertising.

Maybe that's you.

I'll start with the upside. I darkly suspect advertising is a hell of a lot more fun than crime-scene cleanup, septic-system pumping, or money laundering, although I've never tried those alternatives. Maybe I'd be pleasantly surprised and would've found them easier.

Brand building isn't always easy.

Advertising naturally attracts some of the most fabulously talented and fucked up individuals you're likely to meet anywhere this side of the carnival midway. Self-indulgent artists. Sociopaths. Saints. Out-of-the-box thinkers and whip-smart strategists. Brilliant minds who can crack the most difficult codes but can't seem to cross the street without being plowed over by a municipal trash truck.

Which brings me back to my reasons for writing this book. I've written it to help you recognize the traps, the pitfalls, and the early warning signs of things going awry.

To help you get in, and reach the other end of your journey with your sanity intact and your conscience clear.

Chew With Your Mind Open is for those looking to take brands into the future. For the wide-eyed ad school grad entering the real world where the stakes are higher and the opportunity to do kickass work, lower. For undergrads who may not have deep enough pockets to get a four-year degree or attend a portfolio school.

And yes, if it means quadrupling sales, this survival guide is also for the casual observer who'd rather not squander his or her peak earning years in the ad racket, but wouldn't mind having a voyeuristic peek behind the curtain and a few stories to share.

Whether you're just starting out, stuck in a dead-end job, or simply take pleasure in experiencing train wrecks without needing the jaws of life to extract you, welcome.

CWYMO is loaded with tips and tricks that have worked for me and actual experiences. You'll find an absence of hypothetical bullshit or abstract theories. This book is my take on how to survive the slings and arrows of a business where winning and losing are inevitable and fragile egos are par for the course.

Welcome to the soft pink underbelly of advertising creativity.

I hope to help creatives recognize occupational quicksand and toxic people for exactly what they are. Time bandits, ready to cramp your style, sully your name, and take undue credit for your work.

Used judiciously, this book will help you focus on the only thing that matters.

The work.

I was lucky. I had a secret weapon. A 24/7 career coach who understood creativity and brand-building better than 99% of the population. I had mentorship from a father who never let his famous advertising name go to his head or mine.

I had Guy Day in my corner.

My father was the latter half of Chiat/Day, a once-small Los Angeles creative boutique that is now an 800 lb. global gorilla with a longer name and a holding company pulling its strings.

The work my dad's agency produced before he bowed out was the stuff of legend.

Porsche ads as meticulously crafted as the cars. Nike Summer Olympics work that painted the town in giant murals with no words, just a swoosh for a logo. California Coolers work that celebrated surf culture and garnered the respect of real surfers. Pizza Hut commercials that made you think, and somehow managed to skirt the typical food-commercial clichés. And let's not forget the advertising commercial that forever changed Super Bowl ads as we know it, the "1984" Apple Macintosh launch spot.

If you had tried to give my dad credit for the work coming out of Chiat/Day, L.A. in the eighties, he'd deflect it, and point to his spotlight-loving New York-based partner, Jay Chiat, or direct your attention to L.A.'s long-standing creative guru, Lee Clow.

He'd credit everyone but himself. And that's what made him such a unique human being. He refused to buy into the hype, his own, or his agency's. He was modest and believed in talented people, and in pushing them to execute to the fullest of their abilities. He drove his clients to great work by earning their trust and taught me to do the same.

He helped me in ways I believe I can now help you on the off chance you're one parent short of having unlimited access to advertising royalty, which my father would never lay claim to despite history suggesting otherwise.

My dad let the work do 99.9% of the talking and had an uncanny knack for holding feet to the fire when it counted. He also possessed a remarkable tolerance for eccentrics as long as they were committed to the work and had integrity.

What my dad respected above all else was disciplined thinking in its most creative form.

He provided a metric-ton of savvy advice to me throughout my career. But like many sons before me, I didn't always listen. I stepped in a fair amount of drama, and chances are you will, too, if you make advertising your vocation.

If you're fast on your feet, have talent, and are able to navigate the shifting tides and the oversized personalities, you can have a great career in advertising.

You've just got to be smart about it.

After all, the sharks outnumber the flotation devices, and given all the distractions, it's easy to lose sight of the real prize.

Simply put, the work is the only thing that is left when the tents come down and clowns head for a new town.

Throughout my career, I've been fortunate enough to work with a lot of talented folks and on a handful of great brands, some global, and others regional. I've had a hand in steering Land Rover, Toyota, Rolling Stone, Microsoft, and Diesel, as well as regional accounts like Shiner Beer, Frost Bank, Whataburger, and Wyoming Tourism, to name just a few.

Many people have graciously shared their wisdom and insights with me and made me a better problem-solver for it.

Others had the opposite effect. They're the fucktards and dillweeds who rained on my parade and took perverse pleasure in watching me flounder.

You'll meet both types throughout these pages. The altruistic team players, the hapless idiots, and the self-proclaimed geniuses.

Hindsight being what it is, I couldn't have accomplished what I have without every one of them, although I'd have been hard-pressed to admit it at the time. For the record, I have a hard time giving jerks credit for helping me. But in all fairness, I'll try to take the high road and do so.

Throughout my career, I've served as a brand steward, a pitchman, a foot soldier, a general, and a mentor, both in and out of the full-time trenches. I've helmed creative departments, big and small. I've been hired, fired, laid off, and paid off. I've worked for small independent agencies and global behemoths, as both a freelancer and a full-time employee and held titles ranging from junior copywriter to chief creative mentor.

Managing the inmates was never my favorite part of the job, but a willingness to do so allowed me to reach the higher elevations on the org charts and salary levels that allowed my wife to be a stay-at-home mom, and a serial entrepreneur, which is a story for another day.

I thank my stars that I was able to remain a working writer every step of the way.

So, why the hell should you listen to me? Because I'm a survivor. Because I still love what I do and am still doing it. Because despite the bullshit, I'd do it all over again given the chance.

Advertising is one of the most exhilarating rides I know of. It's rarely dull. If you've got talent, it's a great way to make a living. Seeing an idea spring from your imagination into a multimedia campaign that touches millions is nothing short of intoxicating.

Branding is a craft requiring skill, resilience, experimentation, and savvy. No matter how hard the bean counters of the business try to make it an exact science, advertising is not one. I'm three-plus decades of living proof that the right advice can make a difference.

Unfortunately, on-the-job training is less prevalent in our business today. Too many agencies expect university advertising programs and portfolio schools to do all the hard work for them. And with everyone being so damn busy, internships can be a tough row to hoe. Algorithms now vet resumes and it's getting harder than ever to look a potential employer in the eye. No marketing degree or ad agency can completely prepare you for what lies ahead.

That's where this book comes in.

My experiences could keep you from rolling a steady string of embarrassing gutter balls. I won't attempt to teach you how to concept. But I might just be able to help you read the room and properly assess situations. To clear hurdles and overcome perplexing barriers. To remove a few of the cogs that stand between you and doing your best thinking.

The advice in this book will help you survive and succeed if you're willing to soak it up. None of it comes with a guarantee. All I can tell you is that it worked for me and it could work for you, too.

My content is broken down to make light skimming easier. I get it. Not everyone wants to endure a bunch of blood-and-guts war stories. But those who do will have a few good tales to share and learn all too well that nobody's perfect, particularly me.

Each chapter of CWYMO is broken into three distinct acts to help ease your digestion:

Act One: **Subject** — A topic is identified, and advice is provided like complementary breath mints at a speed-dating event.
Note: *Never say no to a breath mint.*

Act Two: **Storytime** — A true story is shared, demonstrating the value of heeding good advice or the dangers of ignoring it. Occasionally, I share more than one story. Feel free to skip this soft center of each chapter if you want to stick with the actionable advice. It'll certainly spare myself and others some embarrassment.

Act Three: **Food for Thought** — An emergency punch list of workarounds, tips, and tricks, relating to the subject. Think of this section as your advertising survival guide *Cliff Notes.*

A couple of disclosures seem fitting before I set fire to the dumpster.

Disclosure One: some of the names I've used are real. They're the good ones. Real-life mentors. The patron saints of my career. Other names have been changed, based on legal counsel and my desire not to rub an entire block of salt into the fragile egos of miscreants who took pleasure in slowing my roll.

Disclosure Two: if you're easily offended by coarse language, political incorrectness, or a writing style that occasionally trots the good lady of grammar out in a micro mini, visit your nearest HR department and lodge a formal fucking complaint.

Have them put it on my tab.

DON'T LET YOUR FIRST JOB **BE YOUR WORST JOB**

You've received an offer? Awesome.

It's proof you've built a solid portfolio and that you're not coming across as an ax-murderer. Not yet, anyway. But that offer is no guarantee you've found the right gig. Temper your enthusiasm. As the legendary Groucho Marx once said, "I wouldn't join a club that would have me as a member."

Groucho may have had a point there, and one here as well. Don't take the first job you're offered unless it fits most, if not all of your criteria.

It pains me to admit it, but I made that mistake. I accepted the first job offer I got before I could consult with my dad, whose wisdom and experience as an agency owner could have offered me some perspective. But no, I jumped at the first job offer I got, and while it wasn't the worst job in the world, I now know I could have done better.

In fairness to my first employer, he probably could've found a more suitable candidate, too.

Let's just say the first agency I worked at wasn't exactly setting the world on fire. Within months, I could read the writing on the wall and it was no better than my own writing at the time, which left a lot of room for improvement. My boss was a dolt, and I was right up there with him for taking the gig.

I left before my first anniversary and frankly, a couple more moves like that, and my resume would have painted me into a corner I never would've gotten out of.

NOBODY WANTS TO HIRE A JOB-HOPPER.

Granted, you may be quaking in your boots that you'll never find a job, let alone a good one. I felt the same way, despite having a legendary dad running a great agency with his name on the door. That said, I should have listened to him. I should have been more selective about my first full-time gig. I should have waited for the right job.

An outside observer could argue that I should have begged my way into Chiat/Day and taken the humiliation of being a guy who got there the easy way. Not this bonehead. I was determined to make it on my own.

I was so damned anxious to get in on my own merit that I accepted the wrong gig. It was my first big mistake. Within months, I was digging through the vocational dumpster for a new gig as if it were a retainer left on a melamine cafeteria tray.

DON'T SCREW YOURSELF OUT OF A GREAT FIRST GIG.

A solid boss at a decent agency should be your goal at the very minimum. Someone with legit mentoring skills, who makes time for you rather than treating you like a grunt, an inconvenience, or a necessary evil.

Find a boss who is willing to invest in building your skillset and enjoys helping others grow. Great bosses do exist. I've discovered that a lot of the time, they're not necessarily the most legendary creatives. They're willing and capable of doing the job they've been tasked with, which is directing creative and sharing the opportunities with others.

I've been fortunate and had a handful of really good bosses. They're definitely worth finding, and the sooner the better for the sake of your own sanity and portfolio.

Unfortunately, many bosses look at managing as an imposition, and it can be, but that's the job a creative director signs up for. Avoid any boss who appears overwhelmed or resents having to manage or give direction.

If you aren't getting solid creative direction, you're going to be in a world of hurt.

With that in mind, it doesn't hurt to pepper your potential employer with questions. Try and spread your questions out among everyone you meet, so it doesn't appear that you're staging an inquisition.

A FEW QUESTIONS WORTH ASKING BEFORE ACCEPTING ANY JOB.

- How much work moves through your department?
- Who would I report directly to?
- Where are the best opportunities for great creatives to shine?
- What is your biggest challenge to doing great work?
- How do I advance?
- How can I help you succeed?
- How will my success be measured?
- Will I get a shot at the good assignments if I prove myself?
- Who are your best employees and why?

Pay careful attention to the answers. If a potential boss seems put off by your questions, he or she may have no intention of offering you anything resembling real opportunity.

If your interviewer is stressed out or in a big hurry to fill the position, he or she may be like that all the time. Bosses who are martyrs or artiste types can be a real pain in the ass to work for and saddle you with bad habits that can be hard to break.

SOME OF THE BIGGEST NAMES IN THE BUSINESS CAN BE AMONG THE SMALLEST PEOPLE YOU'LL EVER MEET.

Sheer talent doesn't make someone a competent manager or an admirable human being. It merely makes them talented. No more. No less. What they say about misery, love, and company is true.

But that doesn't mean that you should actively avoid going to work for a vastly talented person who is mercurial, or egomaniacal if you go into it with your eyes wide open. As long as you're not being physically or emotionally harmed, it's a great way to develop a thicker skin and prepare you for a future in a business that often tolerates aberrant and eccentric behavior from its star players.

Great skills don't always come attached to great people, and vice versa. Oftentimes, the most redeeming quality of a boss who is difficult is that the bar is set high, and that isn't a bad standard to have your work held to.

STEVE JOBS USED TO MAKE HIS PEOPLE CRY.

To my way of thinking, the infamous Steve Jobs was a self-absorbed jerk who also happened to be a genius. He legitimately changed the world to be sure, but at what cost to those around him? While at Apple, he would park his car in the handicapped spots in front of headquarters, sometimes taking up both dedicated spaces. He had no infirmities to speak of, other than a herculean ego and extreme narcissism.

Jobs used to take credit for other people's thinking and patent ideas without sharing the credit with its originators. He could be downright cruel to his underlings. He wasn't a great father to his first child. Yet no one would contest that Jobs was a genius.

I could never have worked for Jobs -- not that he ever offered-- as I know I wouldn't have survived his constant bullying and badgering. Maybe that speaks to the chinks in my own psyche, but as far as I'm concerned, life's too short for that shit.

SOME OF THE BRIGHTEST PEOPLE YOU'LL MEET CAN BE A NIGHTMARE TO BE TRAPPED IN A BUILDING WITH.

In all fairness, they can be worth it, if you're patient and can accept their eccentricities. If you're gaining valuable experience, learning, and creating great work, it could be worth carrying their baggage, as long as you can handle the ups and downs without having to double down on therapy sessions or becoming clinically depressed.

I've always done my best work for bosses who understood how to delegate and inspire without resorting to intimidation or public humiliation. I want to be challenged, not berated. I prefer well-earned compliments to psychic gut punches.

It's worth recognizing what motivates you to do your best thinking. No boss is perfect. No employee is either. To me, a great boss is someone who builds a better you. So, choose bosses as if your future depends on it.

Because it does.

FIRST THINGS FIRST. LET'S NOT PRETEND THAT YOU HAVE A CLUE.

When interviewing, be honest with yourself and others about your skills and don't bluff about your abilities or overstate your skillset. Never overstate what you can do. Pretending won't impress anyone for long, and it could rightfully result in your ass being handed to you.

Understand precisely what's expected of you and make damn sure that your employer is willing to provide training if you're expected to provide a skill that you don't presently have. When in doubt, ask. If your employer isn't willing to help you hone your skills, find one that will.

Learning to say "no thank you" to the wrong offer is one of the most crucial skills you can master.

DON'T FALL FOR THE CHEAP COLOGNE OF A CHILL HANG SPACE.

Another thing worth saying "no" to is an office that seems too good to be true. Free drinks and snacks, Ping-Pong tables, and curated hang spaces don't improve an agency's creativity. If you derive real satisfaction from doing great work first and foremost, don't let an impossibly cool space sway you. Look at the work, not the office space. Learn to recognize the telltale signs of a sweatshop like free caffeine and a wide assortment of "healthy" snacks. Sure, those all seem tempting. But they could be there to keep you chained to your desk laboring under a nonstop workload.

IT'S THE END OF ANOTHER GRUELING DAY. GET YOUR ASS BACK TO WORK.

If you don't mind long hours and a tough grind, sweatshops can be quite beneficial to your career, particularly in the very beginning. You can learn a ton and rise quickly. But that's not everyone's idea of an ideal gig. If you burn out easily and don't aspire to live at the office, don't pitch your tent at a sweatshop.

You won't be a happy camper for long. So, how do you know a sweatshop when you see one? It's a boot-camp mentality. People work ungodly long hours and walking out before dark is generally frowned upon.

Proceed with extreme caution if that's what you're seeing. Too much perspiration and caffeine, and not enough vitamin D from direct sunlight can be detrimental to your health, your hobbies, your friendships, and your family life, even if the work is top-notch.

In the plus column, however, what you will get is a ton of at-bats. The churn-and-burn pace offers more potential to people really willing to hustle. If you can handle the grind, go for it. The law of averages dictates that you'll get more shots at landing a big idea and get ahead faster by trading a chunk of your life for a tour of duty at a sweatshop.

KNOW WHAT YOU'RE SIGNING UP FOR. SERIOUSLY.

Be realistic about what you want from a first job. Find one that works for you, and think twice before trading everything for advertising immortality. Not everyone wants the same thing from an advertising career and sweatshops aren't for everyone. Unlimited after-hours pizza can turn you into a walking marshmallow.

Full-time employment isn't for everyone. Life is short, and the world is crawling with lonely people who've built epic portfolios. Hey, is that tarnished metal doorstop a 90's Cannes Lion?

IS THE BEST AGENCY FOR YOU NOT AN AGENCY?

You might want to work directly for a company as an in-house creative. Apple, Google, Amazon, or Lyft, for instance. If you're interested in learning a lot about an industry and delving deeply into one industry, an in-house job at a company you admire can be a great option. If you prefer a little more variety in your routine, you might find that an agency is better, as it offers a more diverse roster of accounts and opportunities in different categories.

I can't tell you what's right for you. It depends on who you are and how you are wired. But I can tell you this much: hopping into the sack with the wrong job sucks. The advertising walk of shame is not something you want to experience, whether early or at any point in your career.

The more you understand about a company, its culture and expectations, the more prepared you'll be to make the right decision for you.

And with that in mind, it's Storytime.

I didn't just hit the wall. I threw a chair through it

I once quit a job without having another one and it was a bonehead move. What happened next made an unfortunate situation worse. I accepted a copywriting job on an account that didn't interest me in the least. Granted, it was better than starving to death but not by much.

I was unemployed, having quit my prior job after getting sideways with a boss who in my mind had no business being one. Reality set in faster than Superglue on a kid's fingertip. I'd made a mistake. My wife was working as a photographer's rep at the time so we had some income. Let's just say that our savings account was on the thin side and we had a nut to cover.

Which brings me to the other nut in this story, a charismatic Hungarian creative director who managed to convince me I was the perfect young writer to help him brand a software company with big plans but very little marketing savvy. I didn't know the name Bill Gates from Adam or his software company, Microsoft, and I confessed as much in my interview. As much as I admired the creative director's prior work, every instinct told me to turn the job down.

So, turn it down, I did.

I explained that software didn't interest me, and I feared I'd fail miserably, not being a "techie" by nature or even intellectually curious about the internal workings of software or computers. The creative director had a wicked comeback,"...That's why you'd be perfect for it! You clearly care about your work and I want that level of passion to come through for this brand. I want the work to be passionate, and not overly techie."

Still, I resisted. That's when it happened. The golden cuffs came out. I was offered an additional 20K over the original salary being offered. It was world-changing money to me at the time. I did what any stupid, broke, young creative would do. I assumed the position, and I mean that in more ways than one.

Microsoft nearly crashed my internal hard drive. Frequent trips to Redmond had me presenting to rooms of MBAs, who acted more like intellectual robots than actual human beings. Bottom line? I was not the right guy for the job. I ignored my gut when it was practically screaming at me and now I was getting hosed with alarming regularity. It was like being cast into the role of the big dumb jock in one of those cringe-worthy "Revenge of the Nerds" movies.

Instead of socking the extra money away from day one, I did the exact wrong thing. I bought my first home, against the advice of my dad, who cautioned me that having "fuck you" money in the bank was more important than being a homeowner.

One day at the office, an account guy brought me a piece of my copy that was desperately trying to punch its way into production. I think we were in revision round #17, and I was getting frayed by the endless rounds of client changes on every piece I wrote. Clients who could barely string two non-technical words together were second-guessing every paragraph, every sentence, every word.

Even my punctuation was being dissected by the Micro-bots.

I snapped.

All 6-foot-5 inches of me went ape shit. The account guy scampered from my office before I threw a chair across the room. The chair never returned to Earth. It crashed through the drywall and lodged itself in my office wall like a bad piece of conceptual art. Proposed title? "FFFFFUUUUUUCCCCKKKKK!!!!". Perhaps more to the point, it could have been entitled "The Fireable Offense".

The sound of my tantrum alone kept anyone from investigating immediately. In true Shawshank fashion, I quickly taped a large poster over the hole in my wall and cleaned up the drywall dust off the floor before management could see the carnage. As my jets cooled, word raced through the creative department and folks came by to check my vitals.

Had it not been for the poster, I would have been escorted from the building with all my crap in a cardboard box.

I spent that weekend repairing the drywall by myself and thinking about my decision to take a job I was not well wired for. Sure, I could be a total wimp and claim I got hoodwinked by a smooth-talking creative director, but the truth was worse. I got greedy. I took the check and got precisely what I deserved.

I put my portfolio out and in the process of looking for a more suitable job, I learned something equally valuable. It's hard to find a good gig when you're making more money than your peers and have little to show for it beyond a bunch of trade ads stuffed with tech drivel.

I bit the bullet and took a job that didn't necessarily look like a forward move on paper. But it got me out of the job that was eating my brain and came with a parallel salary. The new opportunity was as an associate creative director on a motorcycle account that wasn't doing great work at the time. A lot of my cohorts had no idea why I'd moved to that agency. I knew the answer all too well. I had a mortgage and my first son was on his way.

I took the ACD title, but not because I wanted the title, or was ready for it.

I got lucky. I found a boss I liked and an art director partner who helped me grow into the expanded role of managing people. Although I landed back on my feet, I learned a lesson.

Golden handcuffs are the Chinese finger traps of creativity.

TIPS **FOR JOB HUNTING**

- A great first job, assuming you perform it well, practically ensures a great second job. Which directly contributes to a better resume.

- Never get charmed into taking a job that doesn't fit your career goals or your interests. It might build character, but it sure as hell won't fill your book with the kind of work you want to be associated with.

- If you don't feel good about the job you're being offered, all the money in the world won't change that fact. Trust your gut and just say no.

- Sweatshops are terrific for some people and terrible for others. If you need time to unwind or do your best thinking when well-rested, think twice about taking a job in a sweatshop, no matter what your friends and colleagues think.

- Working in a sweatshop does have advantages. It can raise your profile quickly and help you establish a strong work ethic.

- If you turn down a job, do it respectfully. The person who makes you the offer may want to hire you down the road, and you never know where he or she might be in the future.

- In-house agencies are a more viable option than ever and can give you deeper insights and valuable category experience. Some impressive work is coming out of in-house agencies these days.

- You might be happier working directly for a tech start-up. It's a surefire way to rack up category experience in an industry that interests you.

- Beware of golden handcuffs. Being overpaid may seem like a good problem to have but it can hamper your ability to change jobs if you're not happy.

- Never throw a chair at a wall or in the vicinity of an account executive. Nobody wants to be known as a hothead.

STANDING OUT, WITHOUT THE EMBARRASSING RESTRAINING ORDER

Pestering creative directors is an art form.

While I don't claim to have mastered it, I've been on both sides of the fence. So, I can at least understand it from each point of view.

You should too.

Creative directors are busy people. Everyone wants a piece of them. It ain't all rainbows and unicorns being pulled in a dozen directions at once. They need to be selective about who gets their time because there typically isn't enough of it to go around.

That said, it's on you to be proactive about getting on a creative director's radar without wasting a whole lot of their time. The squeaky wheels are often the ones who get the choice gigs. It may not be fair, but that's the way it is.

YOU REALLY DO NEED A NEW BEST FRIEND.

One smart tactic for getting your work seen is to befriend the creative director's right-hand person. Admins, creative coordinators, and in-house recruiters often hold the keys to the higher-ups' kingdoms. They often know the CD's schedule better than the creative director does. They also know when there are openings and can share your work at the exact right moment. It's well worth finding out what the creative director likes. Be as friendly as hell to creative coordinators and reciprocate if they're up for helping you get your work looked at. Charm them in un-creepy and inventive ways. Send funny little notes about your employment status like "Day 84. Losing resolve as I transition from Top Ramen to dog kibble." Buy them coffee cards. Just don't overdo it.

A small but thoughtful gesture can go a long way.

If they're not open to engaging in banter with you, find out if you can check back with them and be diligent about doing so. After all, there's no shortage of people looking for opportunities.

IF YOU'RE GOING TO FOLLOW CREATIVE DIRECTORS AROUND, AT LEAST BE SNEAKY ABOUT IT.

Another smart way to get noticed? Use your social media skills. Case in point, the legendary stunt that helped a young copywriter named Alec Brownstein land a job based on a simple human insight. He realized that well-known ad people routinely Google themselves. So, Alec bought Google AdWords key-wording the names of the creative directors he most wanted to work for. If a creative director searched their own name, a promotion for Alec popped up.

Some of the ads cost as little as 15 cents.

The result? He got calls from all but one of his "targets," and two job offers. What Alec did was sneaky, but brilliant. As long as you have the work to back it up, don't hesitate to think intuitively in social media.

CAN I WRITE, CAN I WRITE FOR SPRITE?

Chase Zreet is a talented writer I had the good fortune of mentoring at the beginning of his career. In fact, he had a hand in inspiring this book. But that's another story.

Chase called me one day after meeting an account executive who worked at Wieden + Kennedy/NY while on a camping trip with some buddies. At one point, Chase mentioned he was a huge fan of hip-hop. The AE suggested he should try to get a job working at W+K/NY on Sprite, which was heavily leveraging hip-hop culture at that moment in time.

Chase did more than pull a couple of strings. He wrote an entire rap in the guise of a cover letter and had it professionally recorded. When he called to share it with me, I could tell he'd really worked out the rhymes. It sounded legit, catchy beat and all. I was impressed that Chase had really gone for it. I encouraged him to push it even further. I coaxed him to show up at their office in the guise of the character he'd created. I suggested he try to make the local news or perform the rap in Wieden's lobby or in the street in front of their building during lunch hour.

Chase chose a different path.

He convinced a young film director he'd just worked with to shoot his "Cover Letter" as a music video. The result is a video you've got to see to believe. Google "Sprite Cover Letter" and you'll get a sense of just how much web traction and momentum Chase created for himself.

Chase was contacted by Wieden+Kennedy/NY, as well as a handful of recruiters from other agencies. His cover letter to Wieden+Kennedy and the Sprite team had 651,000 views on Vimeo, 49,500 upvotes on Reddit, and garnered thousands of comments as of this writing, mostly from people pulling for him to get the Sprite gig.

Once the video went viral, Chase snagged interviews and scored job offers from multiple agencies, and some very good ones. Zreet did what most creatives haven't got the courage and audacity to do. He went for it full Monty.

He shot the ball from midcourt and found the net. Wieden+Kennedy hired him.

THERE'S A REASON WHY TRAINWRECKS MAKE THE EVENING NEWS.

Kathy Hepinstall is a truly brilliant copywriter, creative director, and published novelist and we've been friends for years. She's hands down one of the most talented creatives I've ever met. Howlingly funny. Self-effacing. Creatively savvy. She can write circles around most writers, present company included.

Kathy once attempted a stunt on the front steps of Wieden+Kennedy/Portland that almost got her carted off to a psych ward. If she'd pulled it off, it would have been strange but wonderful. Sadly, it turned out to be awkward and missed the mark.

Kathy swung and missed in front of the entire agency. But she still managed to make an indelible impression. Dan Wieden hired her freelance. Once he got a look into her fertile mind, she became a permanent member of Wieden's freelance pool.

Kathy ended up doing career-defining work for Wieden+Kennedy -- all because she was willing to ride a white horse onto the steps of one of the greatest agencies in the world and beckon its namesake to ride off into the sunset with her.

Kathy's epic promotional fail preceded her well-deserved success. I only wish my own disasters were so successful.

IF YOU WANT TO BE DIFFERENT, DO IT WELL.

Here's another example of how to hang it out there. A batch of portfolios came into an agency I worked at before websites were the way work was shared. We had a mid-level writer opening at the time. I was low on the totem pole and had no authority to influence hires.

But I constantly looked at the portfolios and found Jeff Nelson's impossible to ignore. It was a powder blue Samsonite suitcase that stood out from the sea of black, zippered, standard-issue portfolio cases. When I cracked open his Samsonite, there, along with his work, were a pair of fresh whitey-tighties, a toothbrush, and a tube of Crest toothpaste.

I never forgot that book. Not only was his work good, but Jeff leaned into his willingness to pull long hours memorably. I met with Jeff and while I wasn't in a position to hire him, I applauded his effort and added him to my personal Rolodex.

What Alec Brownstein, Chase Zreet, Kathy Hepinstall, and Jeff Nelson did was refuse to be ignored. So, hang it out there. Dare to be noticed. Take risks. The risks may end up being rewarded.

Timing and circumstance are important factors, too. But my point to you is simple. Fortune favors the bold.

A sense of humor and being in the right place at the right time can also land you a job if you don't take exception to your work being shown to a creative director by a naked woman masquerading as you.

Just ask Sariah Dorbin.

It's Storytime.

The "birthday suit" surprise

Back in my Della Femina days, we lived in an era before HR managers and political correctness ruled the world. The shit we used to get away with is mind boggling. What we did for an ECD's birthday is no exception and is now part of L.A. advertising lore.

A young writer named Sariah Dorbin was scheduled to interview at our agency. We intercepted our candidate as she stepped into the lobby, and shared our wicked little scheme with her. The entire creative department had chipped-in to fund the elaborate hoax and our creative administrator, Louise, was in on it, too.

Sariah willingly complied. Per our plan, we borrowed her portfolio and stashed her in an empty office and brought in our decoy.

Moments later, Louise led a fully clothed stripper into the corner office, quickly introducing "Sariah" and asked her if she needed water or coffee. Our bogus "Sariah" asked our soon-to-be victim if he had a cassette deck, explaining she'd just produced a radio campaign that she was really proud of and wanted to share it with him. He didn't and asked Louise to track one down.

Louise returned with a boombox, plugged it in, and left the room, shutting the door behind her.

The creative department had their ears pressed up against the corner office's walls. Music started blasting. Moments later, he screamed in horror, "Louise, get in here!!!!"

The entire creative department flooded into his office to find our horrified boss and a woman wearing little more than a mischievous smile.

We all had a good laugh at our embarrassed ECD's expense, and he rightfully told us we were a bunch of raging assholes. He then asked the obvious. "So, where the hell is the real Sariah Dorbin?"

Louise led her in, along with a birthday cake, and we all sang "Happy Birthday" to a great boss.

Sariah's interview was a short one. Our fearless leader had just one question. "So, Sariah, I hope you still want to work at Della Femina?" "Yes, I do..." "Great, you're hired."

The real Sariah started two weeks later and was a great addition to our merry little band of misfits. And as irony would have it, she was not only a great thinker, but also quite a stylish dresser.

FOOD FOR THOUGHT

TIPS FOR INTERVIEWING, AND GETTING NOTICED

- Make yourself impossible to ignore. Get to know the CD's assistants, befriend employees, research the CD's hobbies. Personalize a promo specifically to them.

- Be willing to hang it out there if your book is really good. Embarrassing yourself will almost surely get you remembered. But do so within reason. Keep in mind that what flew two short decades ago would now get you arrested. Be bold, but avoid being socially insensitive or it could have the exact opposite effect. You wouldn't want to wind up in the hoosegow with the town drunks.

- Be nice to personal assistants and look for small ways to reward them for helping keep you on their boss's radar. Flowers. A thoughtful note. A Starbucks card. But don't overdo it. It's intended as a small token of appreciation, not a bribe.

- Always follow up with thank-you notes to anyone who helps get you an interview. Keep 'em short and genuine.

- If you've got a big personality, use it to your advantage. Do something audacious that you won't live down anytime soon.

- If you're not a naturally gregarious person, make your thinking stand out. Do something subtle, but really smart. Social media is a great place to get noticed.

- Remember that creative directors have busy jobs. Value their time and plan any personal promotion accordingly.

- Timing is everything. Strike when there are openings. After a new account win, for example. Or if an existing client announces a new product or service.

- Familiarize yourself with the past work of the person interviewing you. Drop a compliment, so they know you took the time to research them.

- Don't wait for busy advertising creative directors to find you. Be proactive. Get on their radars in interesting ways. Turn the tables.

- By all means, keep your clothes on. Sending a stripper to impersonate yourself in an interview would be a terrible idea today. Look for a way to stand out that won't usher in a network-wide policy in your honor or land you on the FBI's "persons of interest" list.

BIG SHOPS vs. SMALL SHOPS vs. **SHOPS THAT AREN'T SHOPS AT ALL**

Where should you start your advertising career? You'll find numerous options. Opportunities come in all shapes and sizes nowadays. So do agencies and companies looking for creatives to help shape their brands.

Choosing the right path can be a challenge.

In this chapter, I'll hit on the pros and cons I've personally experienced working at agencies big and small. I'll also shed some light on the idea of going to work in-house for a company, which has become an increasingly attractive and viable option for many creatives these days.

LET'S START WITH "BIGGER," AND WE'LL WORK OUR WAY DOWN TO WHAT I CONSIDER "BETTER."

I've hitched my wagon to major brands at some of the biggest agencies in the country. This brings me to one of the big advantages of working at a large agency. Big brands are more likely to have big budgets. And the bigger the budget, the better production values and directorial talent you'll have access to.

Larger agencies also offer more structure as well, if you like that sort of thing. Odds are you'll have a larger pool of employees to learn from. Which can be good or bad, depending on those people.

Most large clients have more rodeos under their spurs and require less hand-holding, but they can also be saddled with an aversion to risk and be a roadblock to producing great work. Unfortunately, larger clients can be more concerned with protecting their asses than producing great work.

All told, the politics of larger agencies and conservative clients can make for less than an optimal breeding ground for inventive thinking. At the same time, I've had the luxury of great relationships with big clients and access to bigger production values, which made some of my best work possible. But more times than not, it was the inescapable politics of the big agency game that I never much cared for.

I've always been drawn to smaller agencies, even though their budgets tend to be smaller.

SMALLER AGENCIES CAN OFFER YOU BIGGER OPPORTUNITIES.

Smaller agencies are often easier to navigate and usually attract less political bullshit, such as titles and pecking orders peppered with self-serving schmucks.

Small agencies can teach you skills larger agencies can't. They're typically scrappier and move faster. You have to be more inventive and able to leverage smaller budgets into bigger ideas. Smaller agencies can help you develop strong problem-solving skills that don't lean on bloated budgets. There are also fewer layers to fight through. Smaller shops often run leaner, so they favor people who can tackle a broad range of clients and projects, and execute in all forms of media. In many cases, small shops are willing to invest in smaller brands that wouldn't be profitable at larger agencies.

Shiner beer and Central Market are perfect examples. In the beginning, McGarrah Jessee treated both accounts as investments and creative opportunities. In return, these accounts provided the agency with the chance to produce campaigns that won awards and garnered industry buzz. True, they weren't hugely profitable. But they allowed our creative group to strut their stuff and helped the agency build a reputation for smart, well-crafted work.

I've always enjoyed the challenge of helping smaller clients take on the big boys and that's why I have a personal preference for smaller agencies. Challenger brands are naturally attracted to smaller shops and often willing to do more daring and interesting work with their smaller budgets, which leaves less room for flabby thinking.

DON'T RULE OUT IN-HOUSE.

While the final option is one I haven't actually experienced firsthand, it's certainly worth considering. You can work in-house for a company, gaining valuable category knowledge and experience by being embedded within one company, which can give you access to the movers and shakers and allow you to be a part of their corporate culture.

Google, Lyft, Apple, Amazon, and any other number companies are redefining what's possible from in-house teams. One of my favorite Super Bowl spots of 2018 was produced by Amazon's in-house agency for Alexa, proving that some companies feel no need to tap traditional agencies to produce high-level branding. The star-studded spot, a collaboration between D1, Amazon's in-house agency, and London production house Lucky General, looked like it came from one of the world's top creative agencies. In reality, it was the first-ever Super Bowl commercial for both parties.

Today, many tech-driven companies are open to rewriting the rules and shifting the paradigms, so you can try things that might never fly at a conventional, multi-layered agency. Plus if you get an in-house position early and provide valuable foundational thinking, you could find yourself in a position to rise fast and be seriously influential as the company grows.

You might even receive stock options as part of your compensation, or a bonus structure that gives you a piece of the action for accepting a salary that treats you as both an employee and an investor. Just make damn sure the company's core values are a good fit with your own. Given that you'll only be working on one brand, if it fails in the marketplace, it can cost you on many levels.

Net-net? Choose the companies you spend your time with very carefully. Never go to work or allow yourself to be stuck on an account that violates your ethics. To thy own conscience be true. And with that, it's time to tell you about my first job in advertising. At a small agency. A really small agency. Cue the synthesized trumpets. The real ones were too expensive.

It's Storytime.

I started at the best little agency in Southern California

I should probably clarify that. I started my career at the best little agency on Robertson Blvd. To further clarify, it was the best little agency on Robertson Blvd. between Santa Monica and Melrose. Okay, it was the only agency on the block. Granted, it was a great place to learn a few skills without being a total embarrassment to my father's good name. But as a place for a young writer who had a lot to learn, it had some significant challenges.

Its owner, for starters.

Elephant-in-the-room time. You may wonder why I didn't wrangle a job at my dad's agency. Fair question. I was determined to not beg for a job at Chiat/Day and I know my dad understood that from the get-go. While I received gobs of great counsel from him, it was never my goal to leverage my way into a gig by begging Lee Clow for a job at the shop that carries my last name. Others might have played their hand differently, but not me.

My first job was offered to me on the strength of a decent portfolio I cobbled together as a student at the Advertising Center in Los Angeles, one of the very first ad schools. Advertising Center offered training from instructors who worked full-time at agencies in and around Los Angeles. I wouldn't put it on par with today's VCU or any of the country's other top advertising programs, but it proved worthwhile by getting me hired.

In fairness to the agency owner who took a chance on me, some very good people had passed through his agency. In fact, a talented art director friend of mine who also got his start there fell for the same line I did. "You know, some damn good creatives have worked here." While true, the owner didn't have a very good answer as to why they were no longer there.

The agency didn't have a creative director on staff and the inmates basically ran the creative department, which had a naive appeal to me at first blush. No higher-ranking creative was hoarding the best assignments. It was a level playing field staffed by lower-wage newbies, and enough work flowed through the agency to have two separate creative teams, a couple of young account executives, and office space with a back deck that overlooked a park in the heart of West Hollywood's Boystown. Never a dull moment.

It seemed like a perfect agency to learn the ropes without being shit-canned. In retrospect, we managed to squeak out some pretty good ads in the time I was there, despite a business model that operated without a creative director. I'll call the owner Goofus for the sake of this story, but it's worth mentioning the handle applied as much to me for taking the job.

The truth hurts.

One day, I got a panicked call from Goofus, who came up through the business as an account guy. Goofus had scheduled a new business pitch for a small fashion retailer and had forgotten all about it. Complete brain fart. We had a client coming in the next day to see spec creative and I was summarily informed that I'd be pitching the work.

What work?

I nearly soiled my 501s when Goofus continued, "We'll just have to come up with something." "We'll"? Yeah, right. My entry-level mind was reeling. I reverted to my secret weapon, having no other choice. I called my dad and explained the situation. "Your boss is a Dolt, Cam. Here's what you're going to do. Ask your boss if he has a case study in the same category." Luckily, he did.

My dad continued, "...you're going to introduce yourself and tell the client that if their brand is going to truly stand for something, you need to know what that something is. Then you're going to warn the client they're going to see a lot of shitty ideas from other agencies that won't be right for the brand. You're going to call bullshit on the other agencies for treating their brand like a commodity. Then you're going to break out the case study your agency has and tell him why that work was truly effective for the client."

The next day, Goofus came in expecting to see work. We didn't have any. I outlined our game plan without telling him I'd been coached. The owner was flabbergasted but knew we didn't have time to do anything but dust off the case study. A couple of hours later, the Politix men's clothing clients were seated across from us in our conference room. Three middle eastern gentlemen would soon be opening a men's clothing boutique in Westwood, a high-profile shopping district near the UCLA campus people flooded to on weekends. It was a great location and their clothing was really interesting.

I stood before the client and railed on any agency who pretended to know what to do on behalf of a client without understanding the brand's vision. I explained that we wanted to know their story before we proposed any solutions. Goofus took the client through our case study for Ditto Jeans. The work was quite good, and the Politix clients seemed genuinely impressed. We spent the remainder of our meeting taking copious notes and hearing about the Politix brand's vision.

The next day, the client called and told us we were dead right. Nothing they'd seen from the other agencies had captured the essence of their brand. Not even close. They awarded us their business.

The work we did for Politix ended up being the best campaign I got out of my first job at the agency, winning awards for the print, outdoor, and radio. The Politix experience convinced me that presenting one's case with confidence can be every bit as powerful as any speculative campaign.

It also convinced me we'd gotten very lucky and that my days weren't long for the first job I'd taken without a creative director who knew the drill.

I suppose my love of small agencies started right there and then. As did my belief in understanding a brand before attempting to come up with ideas for it. I was thankful I'd been able to interface directly with clients but knew I had to find a better learning environment.

If I continued to work with Goofus, I knew it would be to my detriment. I needed a seasoned creative director like nobody's business. There were enough dolts in the ad world already.

TIPS FOR FINDING THE RIGHT GIG

- There is no such thing as a perfect agency or a perfect first job. Find the best position you possibly can, whether it's at a big shop, a small one, or in-house at a company and learn everything you can.

- Bigger agencies afford you access to budgets. You can think on a grander scale and if you sell a grand idea, access better production values.

- Having some small agency experience can make you less dependent on production values and make you a scrappier problem solver.

- Not everyone has to be the next Lee Clow. You can have a fulfilling and successful ad career without working for a big-name agency. Find your agency comfort zone and be true to it.

- Don't rule out in-house gigs. They may lead to interesting opportunities and offer stock options or other incentives tied to growing the brand. Never underestimate the value of stock options.

- Small agencies are more likely to allow younger creatives to present their work, and that's a skill worth developing that will serve you throughout your career.

- If you're new to advertising and working without a creative mentor, you're frankly doing yourself a disservice. Find a great creative director and learn as much as possible.

DARWIN WAS RIGHT. ONLY THE FITTEST PORTFOLIOS SURVIVE

It doesn't matter if you look like Brad Pitt, smell like an ocean breeze, and sell yourself better than Bill Clinton. You're only as good as your work. In this business, there's nothing more important than building a strong portfolio. Easier said than done, but entirely worth it.

A great portfolio paves the way for a promising future. If you produce enough good work, it serves as an impressive calling card to the strongest agencies when you're ready to make your move. Having strong work is your best bet for keeping food on the table especially in a down economy. Tightening and refining your portfolio is a job that never ends. That's part of your evolution. Always be brutally honest with yourself about the strengths and weaknesses of each piece in your portfolio and don't be afraid to pull the runt from the litter when adding new work.

Developing a mercenary mindset towards your work will separate you from the pack. Never show shit, no matter how big the client is or how famous their brand may be. I don't care if the production values are amazing. If the idea sucks, it will only bring your portfolio down. The worst piece in your book could be the first piece someone looks at. Why take that risk?

NO PIGS ALLOWED. AND SLAP SOME DAMN LIPSTICK ON EVERYTHING ELSE.

I'm busy. You're busy. The entire stinkin' universe is busy. Don't be too busy to keep your website current. Put it on your list of mandatories, like doing your timesheets more than once a month. Yes, it sucks. But it sucks even more to be caught unprepared when opportunity knocks.

Organize your work. Control the flow. Your best ideas should be the first and last thing a potential employer sees. Great, good, great, good, great, great, great. No additives or unnecessary fillers.

Show only your very best work. Not the newest thing, not the flavor-of-the-month stuff, not the celebrity-voiced deal you churned out last week. If you're on the fence about a piece, don't show it. Never confuse execution with concept. Resist the temptation to pad your book. If you've got high-dollar production values, but a concept that's less than stellar, hold it for another discussion.

If a potential employer asks about your production experience, that gives you the perfect opening to share well-produced pieces that aren't necessarily your best concepts. You can put your work in context while adding any necessary caveats. A simple disclaimer can go a long way towards demonstrating your judgment.

Which brings up another important point. If you know who's going to interview you, be sure to do your homework. Research the person. Familiarize yourself with their work. To the degree that you can, tailor your pitch accordingly. If your interviewer has made a name for his or herself doing kickass print, start with your tastiest print ads. If they're well-known for humor, put your funniest work first. If they've won a ton of awards for their broadcast, show your TV and radio first, assuming you have some. If they're particularly adept in digital or social, lead with that.

Think of it this way. If someone only skims through your work, how do you make sure your best stuff is seen? Granted, you can't control the order that people look at your work on your website but you can stack the odds in your favor by using hierarchy to your advantage. Start strong. End strong. Don't show shit, under any circumstance.

AD SCHOOL ROCKSTARS TAKE NOTE: YOU'RE BEING CONSIDERED AS AN OPENING ACT.

Think your shit doesn't stink? That can pose a real problem to potential employers. No matter how good your entry-level portfolio is, the stakes are about to become higher and the bullseye smaller. Succeeding in the real advertising world requires a different set of skills than it does in school. It's trickier than just inventing nifty shit. In many cases, it comes down to how well you can continue to evolve an existing campaign and think within the client's box.

My point here is simple. It's no longer just a matter of coming up with the most creative idea without any guidelines. Suddenly, you're servicing a real client and an agency with a larger agenda. You've got to be strategic and choose your battles. It's a delicate balancing act for ad agencies. The work's important, but then so is a solid working relationship with the client.

Packing your portfolio with the coolest shit on the planet is not necessarily an employer's agenda. Agencies are expected to meet business goals, and in many cases, use metrics to measure their success. Beware, not all agencies consider great work a priority over delivering on those metrics. Everything can be measured to death these days, and in many cases is.

If you want to be great at what you do, realize that the target isn't an arbitrary one. You've got a needle to move. It's a business. Learn to think like a consumer and charm like an ambassador. Keep your eye on the prize and be smart about building your client's brand. If you can be the type of creative who cares about making work that's both good and effective, you'll do better off in the long run and spend less time butting heads.

A great portfolio attached to a person who understands that he or she still has a lot to learn is a powerful combination. It's one thing to be a solid opening act. But the main stage is for those who get the big picture and know how to play the big game.

KNOW THY ENEMY.

If you're applying at one of the best agencies, there will likely be a handful of strong job candidates. If you don't get the job, find out who did and look at their work. Befriend them, if possible. There's nothing wrong with having an accurate view of where the agency's bar is set and exactly who meets it.

Always be on the lookout for the very best portfolios. Look at them and ask yourself what makes them rise above. Study the websites of the top candidates coming out of the best ad schools and the galleries of the best work done in the best ad schools and marketing programs. Know who you're up against.

The top portfolios have a distinct advantage. A standout portfolio can even create an opening when the agency doesn't have one. I've seen it happen firsthand.

And with that, it's Storytime.

The portfolio we just couldn't say "no" to

One day at McGarrah Jessee, we got a call from an art director who'd just graduated from Creative Circus, a top ad school. She was recommended to us by none other than Mark Fenske, a talented writer who spent a career doing great work such as the print advertising for Aspen Ski Resort, radio for Wolfgang Puck frozen foods, and the Van Halen "Right Now" video, which was conceived, directed and produced by him when he owned L.A. ad agency, The Bomb Factory. Fenske went on to become a professor at VCU Brand Center in Richmond, Virginia.

The graduate's name was April and she played her hand well. The recommendation of a known creative is a smart way to get on a busy creative director's radar. We had no openings at the time and told her as much but given Fenske's recommendation, we told her we'd be happy to take a look at her work. The date and time were set, and April showed up right on schedule. She explained to my creative partner, James, who met with her first, that she was passing through town before heading to San Francisco for a post-graduation portfolio review.

James gave April a cursory tour of our office before looking at her work. He then dropped April by my office with her portfolio. The first campaign in April's book was smart. No surprise there. Every ad school portfolio starts on a strong campaign unless their work is just plain awful. April's book was the antithesis of awful. Her second campaign was as good as the first, and I patiently waited for the inevitable drop off in the quality of her work as I flipped through her book.

It never happened.

I made it through April's entire book without seeing a single misfire. Not one. Every ad was at least a triple and home runs were scattered throughout her work. Beyond the strong art direction, she had a wide range of tones. The writing was smart as hell. I was floored. My assessment of her work fit into one sentence.

"I'd hire you right now if we had an opening. But we don't." I then asked her about her plans, and she told me that she would be attending a portfolio review in San Francisco the following week, which would be attended by agency talent scouts from all around the country. If I were a betting man I'd have bet the farm that April was a week away for getting a great gig.

I circled back to James.

He was every bit as impressed with her portfolio as I was. He had an idea. "Maybe we should show her stuff to Bryan Jessee", who was a seasoned art director and the agency's cofounder. We poked our heads into Bryan's office and asked if he had time to look at an entry-level book that we both liked a ton. It was a card we didn't play often because Bryan didn't like wasting time. He had other things to do and stated the obvious.

"We don't have an opening."

We countered that we felt the portfolio was worth his time. "Okay, but don't bring her in here. Just bring me the book". We delivered her book to him as April. James, and I continued chatting in my office.

April mentioned that we were only the second agency she'd met with. The Richards Group had offered her a job a week prior, but she wanted to think about it and also attend the portfolio review in San Francisco, hoping it would bring offers. April was from Dallas and wanted to begin her career in a different market. Another smart move on her part. She was keeping her options open.

Bryan Jessee soon poked his head into my office and briefly introduced himself to April. He asked me to step out for a moment.

"Who is this girl? What's her story?"

I told Bryan she'd received a job offer at The Richards Group and that by the end of next week she was likely to have more offers, given that she was due to attend a portfolio event in San Francisco. Bryan was on his way to an event to meet the out-of-town creatives who'd just judged Austin's local ADDY awards. "Don't let her walk out of here. Can you bring her to the event?"

I walked back into my office baffled and awkwardly made the unusual request. "Um, Bryan Jessee wants to know if you can join us at an ADDY event across town?"

April was caught a bit off-guard. I can't say I blamed her. "Sure, I guess that'd be fine." Fast forward to April and Bryan and me in a room full of Austin Advertising Club members and the ADDY show judges from out of town. Bryan pulled April aside, talked to her for all of five minutes, then beelined back over to me.

"Can you go talk to April? I've got to call McGarrah. We need to offer her a job."

I stammered, "But who would we partner her with?"

"Don't promise her a partner. She'll have to float until we win something, and then we'll hire someone for her. Don't let her leave here without accepting our offer. In fact, tell her we'll buy her airline ticket to SF if she skips the flight."

Bryan Jessee called Mark McGarrah. Mark was totally on board.

Little did Bryan know that both James and I had both told April that going to San Francisco before giving The Richards Group an answer was a smart move. Suddenly, here I was trying to convince her that she needed to come to work for us and blow off the flight. To my amazement, April accepted our offer. I later learned that although she was intrigued about working in a larger market, our little agency was on her shortlist.

As I got to know April, she confessed that she had been through a Journalism program at TCU before attending Creative Circus. Suddenly it was obvious why her writing was as good as her art direction. April's TCU Journalism degree led to the humble beginnings of a portfolio and landed her an internship at Disney's in-house studio, Yellow Shoes.

While there, a creative director was nice enough to critique her portfolio, and flat-out levelled with her. He encouraged her to attend Creative Circus if she wanted to compete at the highest level. Instead of getting her feelings hurt, April took that advice and ran with it.

I have no doubt that she made the right decision.

Her book coming out of The Creative Circus was proof-positive. April entered into the business with a great portfolio and her abilities have led her to the best and brightest agencies in the country.

April worked at McGarrah Jessee for almost four years before moving to NY, where BBH and Mother enlisted her talents. She then went on to work at David Baldwin's agency in North Carolina. Today, April's resume includes gigs at Barton F. Graf, Deutsch, Droga5, and ACE Content -- a spin-off of Anomaly. I have no doubt they were as happy to have her on their payroll as we were to have her on ours.

I imagine someday she'll get to San Francisco. And probably own it.

FOOD FOR THOUGHT

TIPS FOR BUILDING A
GREAT PORTFOLIO

- If an interviewer tells you your portfolio needs more work, odds are they're doing you a great favor. Listen carefully to their critique. Take careful notes. Your ability to take it constructively could make a big difference.

- Don't act like a rock star when you come in to show your portfolio. Being likable is as important as being good. A great portfolio attached to a well-grounded person with genuine enthusiasm is a combo few creative directors can resist.

- The recommendation of a tenured creative who knows great work is as good as gold. If your book is well received but there aren't openings, always ask for referrals and use them to open other doors.

- If your initial portfolio isn't rocking anyone's world, retrench and rebuild before wasting any more unnecessary time. No book is perfect. But if you're looking for a great job, making sure your portfolio is in the top-ten percentile is the most viable way to succeed.

- There's nothing more compelling than a creative who already has an offer in hand. But don't bluff in hopes of getting an offer. Advertising is a small business, and nobody likes being conned.

- If your book is getting a good response, be patient, confident, and tenacious about finding the right gig. Your patience will pay off.

- If you're offered a job, ask what you'll be working on and who you'll be reporting to. Weigh both answers carefully. If those you're working with have a history of producing respectable work, it's likely a good opportunity. If not, think carefully before making your final decision.

- Don't be rushed into making a decision. There's nothing wrong with asking for 24 hours to think about an offer. Ask additional questions, if need be, listen to your gut, and by all means, do your homework. The wrong place is a bad place to be.

- Know a couple of good headhunters and stay in contact with them. Things happen fast in this business, and it never hurts to be top of mind.

THERE'S NO DOWNSIDE TO BEING **EVERYBODY'S FRIEND**

Being popular, well-liked, and able to move effortlessly between social circles isn't just important in high school. It's a skill that can put your ad career on the fast track. And yet, for reasons I've never been able to fathom, networking is one of the least used skills in advertising.

If you can master the ability to appreciate those around you, and give them your time and respect, doors will open for you. It's that simple. At the end of the day, everyone likes being appreciated for their skills and their wisdom. Some of the best lessons I've learned were passed on to me by people who felt I was deserving of it. At the very least, I asked about and showed interest in their respective roles.

So, let's talk about the different disciplines of the people who you'll be working with. Or, should you choose to be a pea-brain, the people you'll be working against.

ACCOUNT PEOPLE: STARTING WARS WITH THEM IS LIKE PISSING IN YOUR OWN CUP OF COFFEE.

Many creatives buy into the "us vs. them" myth when it comes to account people. That's a dipshit move. Account people typically have the client's ear and can have a big hand in selling the work. They often understand the clients' goals and expectations better than anyone else in the agency. Unless they draw first blood or are thoroughly incompetent, treasure your account people, and treat them as allies. They're worth spilling your blood for if they're good. If you're smart about it, you can function as a tag team with a good account person when selling the work. You can reinforce the strategy and they can reinforce the creative. It's a great little switcheroo from the all-too-typical presentation process.

If you line up across the ring from your account people, you're signing up for a world of unnecessary pain. They can easily become your worst nightmare if you taunt them without cause.

Face, meet top turnbuckle. Wham.

Account people have one foot in the agency and one foot in the client's boardroom. They're not the enemy. Thinking that they should robotically sell whatever you or your CD deems worthy, now that might just be the real enemy in the agency's presentation process.

Don't blame the account person if your work doesn't sell. Listen to the client's feedback and take it to heart. Adversarial relationships with your account people rarely end well. Unless your account person is feeding you directly into the sausage grinder, you'd be far better off learning to take it like an adult.

If, on the other hand, they're not doing the job of selling your work in client meetings, don't complain to those who can't make a difference. Complain to the person who can: your boss.

Go directly to your boss and present your case. Unless, of course, your boss is part of the problem. If that's the case, you can always hold out hope that karma strikes like locusts and wipes out all the worthless politicians who subsist on a steady diet of capitulation. On second thought, you're probably better off finding a job where the odds aren't hopelessly stacked against you.

ACCOUNT PLANNERS: THEY OFTEN HOLD THE KEY TO DOING THE SMARTEST WORK.

Learn to utilize planners. Their insights can crack a project-wide open. If you can learn to speak their language, everyone in the process will see you as someone who really cares about nailing the brief and understands strategy. And that helps your clients trust your creative instincts.

Account planners are typically extremely bright people, and they can make you look smart, too. If you develop the ability to leverage their insights with your creativity, you will kick serious conceptual ass.

It's never a bad idea to talk to the planner, particularly if the ideas aren't flowing. They'll be able to share stuff with you that may have been left out of the brief for the sake of brevity. Planners can help trigger bigger thinking if you're willing to delve deeper into the strategy than most creatives go. A good planner can function as a third member of the creative team, helping you focus your thinking and tapping into the proverbial mother lode. Insight.

AGENCY HEADS: IT'S SMART TO BE ON GOOD TERMS WITH THE PEOPLE WHO CAN CRUSH YOUR DREAMS.

Depending on your seniority and the size of your agency, you may either have very little interaction with the big guns, or a daily dose of it. Regardless of your rung on the ladder, you can benefit from paying attention to upper management. If you're just coming up in the creative world, observe how they interact with all departments as they move through the agency. The best ones will take the time to acknowledge people in each and every department, and provide a positive vibe in everything they do. That's a good MO to develop for yourself, by the way. Many agency principals keep an eye out for team players. They understand everyone's roles and are in a unique position to expand the roles of others if they like what they see.

Pay particular attention to those who came up through the creative ranks. If they move seamlessly between departments, try to emulate their behavior without being a total apple polisher or a parrot. Presidents and principals can do you a world of good if you respect their role and they see you as providing genuine value to the agency.

CLIENTS; IT'S NOT NECESSARILY YOUR WORK THEY AREN'T BUYING. IT COULD BE YOU.

I cover this vital relationship in greater detail elsewhere, but it bears repeating for the chapter skimmers among us. Before you can reasonably expect to sell your clients good work, you have to sell them on you. After all, you, your partner, your boss, and the account people are pretty much the face of the agency for 90% for the interactions. If you're fortunate enough to present to the client, make sure you're representing yourself, the agency, and the work as effectively as possible.

It's never a bad idea to try and get to know your client beyond your respective roles. Discuss work you're inspired by, and then ask them what kind of work they aspire to do. They just might surprise you.

Ask them about their hobbies. Share yours. Finding common ground early on in the relationship can be a step towards building a solid foundation for greater things. You'll get solid clues into how they think.

A lot of creatives treat their clients as a barrier to great work. While they certainly can be, that's a misguided mentality right out of the gate. The real barrier can be that actual mindset itself.

HERE'S A THOUGHT: GROW UP.

Truth is, the client controls the purse strings. Their billings have a direct effect on the prosperity of your agency. While awards are great, the major players on advertising's stage measure their success by the number of zeroes on the agency's billing statement.

If the clients aren't kept happy, those numbers can dwindle at a rate that will make your head spin. And without paying clients on the ledger, your agency can implode no matter how credible or creative it appears to be on the surface.

Clients are your life's blood. Don't sell them short. Value them. Listen to them. Try to understand what makes them tick and what makes them successful in the eyes of their bosses. If you help them achieve their goals, they'll be far more likely to help you achieve yours. Simply put, a creative who builds bridges as opposed to blowing them up is a valuable resource to both the agency and their clients.

If you can be that type of employee, you'll be one less thing for your creative director to worry about. And one step closer to being irreplaceable. Cha-ching.

CREATIVE DIRECTORS; SCRATCH THEIR BACKS, AND THEY'LL BE FAR LESS LIKELY TO SCRATCH YOU FROM THEIR DEPARTMENTS.

Your immediate boss is in a position to use you in any way he or she sees fit. That goes with the territory.

That said, if you can become a trusted resource to your boss, you'll likely become indispensable.

So how do you accomplish that? Try being the Ray Donovan of your creative department. Fix things. Make messy problems disappear. Become a solution assembly line in the eyes of your boss. Focus on the shit that really matters. The work, the work, and nothing but the work.

Creatives who focus on the work and block everything else out are the ones that managers give the first shot at the best stuff, while the whiners often get tasked with churning out the low-level work. Respect and admiration are earned. If you can make problems go away, you'll become a go-to person. A person your agency taps when the chips are down, or the bases are loaded.

That's the kind of problem-solver we should all aspire to be.

Another mark of a true problem-solver is to not create, produce, or attract unnecessary drama at the office or with the client. If your boss has to follow you around putting out brush fires, your act will wear thin. Trust me, your boss has better things to do than clean up after you.

Why be an ass when you can be an asset?

Don't complain about every partner you're given. Or kvetch that you never get the great assignments. Don't act like a dick around the account people, and treat the client with veiled contempt or arrogance. Put your head down, and attack every assignment as an opportunity, even if it isn't a golden one. If it can't be solved brilliantly, solve it quickly and competently.

Do the job you were hired to do, and you'll likely be top of mind when bigger opportunities arise. If you work hard enough to make yourself indispensable, you will be.

FELLOW CREATIVES: TREADING THE MURKY WATERS OF A CREATIVE DEPARTMENT.

You might think your fellow creatives don't belong on this list because they don't possess a whole lot of power and influence over your career. That's where you're wrong. They are your peers, and, given this age of reality TV shows that vote people off islands for sport, they can be plotting your demise or greasing your success.

Want a comrade for life? Celebrate your colleagues' successes and always support those worthy of your allegiance. Sometimes that means admitting when you've been beaten. Sometimes it means improving someone else's idea. Sometimes it means helping someone else's big idea in small ways. If you handle yourself and others with integrity, your fan base will expand beyond your department. You might even find yourself referred for a better position by those you've helped along the way.

Never underestimate the value of a solid reputation among your peers.

The choice is yours. You can be the subject of bitchy Happy Hour dialogues, or be the one everyone wants to see succeed. How you handle yourself around your peers can make all the difference, and cement your reputation, good or bad.

PRODUCERS: BORROW YOUR SALT FROM THE SEASONED PROFESSIONALS DOWN THE HALL.

A good producer makes everyone's job easier. They know their way around productions, what is and isn't in the bid, and can help you navigate a production with dozens of moving parts. They understand the natural order, even if you don't. Give them the respect and the courtesy they deserve, and they can set you up with the best vendors in the business and make you look good in production, especially if you're inexperienced. There is decorum on every set and unwritten rules you need to be aware of. A producer can help you in that regard and have a strong hand in helping you succeed.

How you treat them can make a tremendous difference.

Respect them and the process. After all, most producers know and appreciate film more than the average bear and the same likely goes for editing, and every other step of the process. Producers are walking encyclopedias of the best production resources. That's their job.

If an agency producer suggests that you watch a director's reel, watch the damn reel. They may be giving you the inside track to a rising star who will soon be on everyone's A-list. They could be sharing a great new film technique with you that you can file away for later use. Or maybe they just want to share something cool with you because you're always cool to them. It's reciprocal. If you see a commercial you dig, a good producer can help you find out who shot it, scored it, edited it, or sound-designed it. They can get you the inside scoop.

And that can help you significantly up your game.

If you're ever given free advice by an agency producer about coaching talent, casting your commercials, interacting with vendors, or even how to dialog with directors while on set, hear them out. Chances are he or she knows something you don't. Since they've probably learned a thing or two about successful communication techniques, they can help teach you the same. They may even be saving special directors or vendors for their favorite creatives who get it – and get them.

There's no reason why you can't earn your way into their inner circle.

HEADHUNTERS: HOLLYWOOD STARS AREN'T THE ONLY ONES WHO NEED GOOD AGENTS.

Having a solid relationship with a reputable headhunter is an extremely wise and worthwhile investment. One good headhunter who believes in you and your work is worth more than all the folks who throw out mass cattle calls on LinkedIn.

Be loyal to your headhunter. At the same time, try to avoid exclusive arrangements. Give them first rights to shop you for all openings, but realize that no headhunter covers the entire landscape, no matter who they are or how well-connected they purport to be.

If a new headhunter approaches you, always tell them if you have a headhunter you trust, but be willing to hear them out. They may have exclusive arrangements with certain agencies and be privy to an opening your current headhunter doesn't know about. If you do get a hot lead from a headhunter you haven't worked with in the past, let your go-to headhunter know about it. That's simple courtesy. If they value your relationship, they'll appreciate your honesty. They'll also work harder on your behalf knowing you're being actively courted by their competitors.

VENDORS: FRIENDS AND FAMILY ASIDE, THEY'RE AMONG YOUR MOST VALUABLE RELATIVES.

A good relationship with outside vendors puts you on solid footing to meet great people you might not otherwise get an audience with. Just remember that no vendor walks the agency asshole around their places and introduces them to their favorite people.The best vendors attract the best agencies. And if you play your cards right, you can meet the people you most want to work with through your vendors. Find out from editors which directors are their favorites and why. Ask them where the best ideas are coming from, who is doing the best music and sound design. Follow their leads to the best work and the people behind it. Vendors are a great source of referrals.

Mutual respect and loyalty are also valuable building blocks throughout your career. If you love working with a certain vendor, request them in the future. It's pretty basic stuff. Champion the people you most respect, and chances are they'll champion you. Tempting as it is, don't gripe about colleagues or work troubles in edit bays or recording sessions. It's a small business, and everyone knows everyone. Loose lips can sink your ship. Keep it professional, enjoy the process, and focus on learning everything you can from the best people in the business.

Your vendors are likely to have solid working relationships with some of the best agencies and companies in town. And that can help advance your career. Holiday vendor parties and industry open houses are valuable networking opportunities. But use caution. Don't be the guy or gal who knocks back a few too many, and runs their mouth in front of strangers.

I'll leave you with one more pearl of wisdom my dad shared with me early in my career. Not everyone is equal in this business. But if you treat everyone as if they are, you will master the art of being on great terms with everyone. And that can set the stage for good things to happen.

Even if you get off to a rough start with someone.

With that in mind, it's Storytime.

Choosing common ground over scorched earth

I once worked with an account supervisor who brought out my worst as a creative director. And I brought out her worst as an account person. From the moment I signed on as Barnhart's executive creative director, Christine and I began locking horns in front of our teams. Neither of us was getting anywhere, and we were making each other and our respective teams miserable.

I felt she was overly analytical and a poor judge of the creative. Christine felt like I was overprotective of my group's thinking and that we were frequently off-strategy. We were driving a stake between our departments and weren't long for each other if something didn't change.

One day, I stepped into her office and asked if we could chat. She was having a bad day. She let her guard down and mentioned she was having issues with her teenage son and couldn't talk with me. I came back later and asked if we could close her door. Instead of diving right into the subject of work, I mentioned that I, too, had a teenage son who was driving my wife and me up the wall. With visible relief, Christine opened up. I listened as a fellow parent, not a creative director. Her issues were nothing my wife and I hadn't seen from our sons. As I shared a few things that had worked for us, she listened with interest. For the first time since joining the agency, I saw Christine in a whole new light.

She was a human being with real-life problems, just like the rest of us. We actually shared a common bond that had nothing to do with advertising. Our respective sons became our bond. We compared notes. We traded advice. We listened to each other. I saw her beyond her job and she saw me beyond mine.

It was a new beginning for us.

Once we'd found our common ground, we soon figured out how to work well with each other inside the walls of the agency. We hatched a plan. If I showed Christine work she was uncomfortable with, she would resist the temptation to pick it apart. Instead, she would simply say "Let's discuss this direction later." That was code. I would circle back to her after the meeting, and we'd have a closed-door discussion that went no further than the two of us in the room. I soon discovered how strategic Christine was, and that she had a knack for predicting the client's pain points.

Once I became comfortable with Christine's private feedback, I was better able to address her concerns one-on-one, rather than in front of my department. Her points were usually quite legitimate, and, when I felt they weren't, I pushed back privately and in a non-combative fashion. We were no longer coming to blows in front of our people. We were getting along, and everyone felt the immediate difference. We were united towards the common goal of creating great work that was both strategic and creative.

Christine ended up being a key to my creative success at Barnhart and ran interference for me with our client like few other account partners I've had. We'd map out our presentations and rehearse during the hour-long car ride to our Wyoming tourism client. It worked like a charm, and the client loved our work and our presentations.

Once Christine and I got on the same page, we crafted genuinely great things together. The work we sold for Wyoming tourism continues to be among my favorite and most effective bodies of work.

To this day, I still call Christine, though we're states apart. I ask about her son and she asks about mine. We share our lives and revel in the fact that neither of our sons succeeded in driving us crazy. I call her my world's favorite account person, and we laugh about the infamous rough patch we put each other through before we found common ground.

The moral of this story? We all have problems, and if you can find common ground with your colleagues, there's no better building block for solving problems. Whether they have to do with advertising or life itself.

NETWORKING TIPS

- Get to know everyone in the agency, and treat people in all departments with courtesy and respect. That doesn't make you a brown-noser. It makes you a team player – and a valued one at that.

- If you can't say something nice about someone, consider saying nothing at all. No one crashes and burns when they take the high road.

- Think of your job as paid tuition for your continuing advertising education. If you're open to it, you'll find the whole building filled with folks who've been to more rodeos than you have. Many of them can help you stay on your horse.

- There's nothing wrong with having a hero, no matter how long you – or they – have been in the business. If you see someone you admire, figure out why. Try to emulate the traits that make them special.

- Never underestimate the value of a one-on-one, closed-door conversation if you've gotten off on the wrong foot with someone. Burnt bridges go nowhere.

- Vendors are a great way to expand your network. Speak highly of them, and they'll likely return the favor while working with other creatives in town.

- Always look for common ground with people you perceive to be your polar opposite. You can learn a lot from them if they're willing to put up with you.

- Agency principals often recognize leadership skills in people long before people see it in themselves. Follow their lead, and they may make you part of the bigger picture in the future.

BRIEFS. THEY'RE NOT JUST WHAT YOU WEAR ON YOUR HEAD AT PARTIES

Most creatives view communication briefs like an AP Calculus class. They approach it with equal parts dread, boredom, and malaise. That's unfortunate. After all, their success is riding on the brief. Without it, you can't create jack.

The brief is your "Star-Spangled Banner." If it isn't performed at the start of the game, you're in for a tough conceptual slog.

Learn to read a brief thoroughly. If it's clear, boiled down, and well done, you should be able to create good work from it. Sometimes you'll need to dig deeper or focus selectively on one support point in the brief.

Isolating one key nugget of insight from pages of information is an important skill to develop.

While every shop uses a slightly different briefing document, they all serve the same purpose. They are created to provide your imagination with the fodder. They define the objective and selling proposition and provide you with background, support points, and inspiration. The brief is your springboard. Dive in. If you aren't finding rich territory, the problem might not be you. It just might be the brief.

NOTHING IS SET IN STONE, INCLUDING THE BRIEF.

Here's the truth. A brief is a guess. An educated guess, to be sure, but a guess all the same. Think of it as your first round of creative. It's open to change and improvement. It's malleable. If you think you can make a brief stronger, sharper, or clearer, go to the account person or the planner, and respectfully share your thoughts.

"This brief is a total piece of shit" is probably not the best choice of words. If you don't respect the thinking behind the brief, the author of the brief isn't likely to respect yours. Nobody hits a home run every time. Time wasted disparaging the brief could be time spent improving it.

If you blindly accept the brief, or, worse yet, choose to ignore it, you're setting yourself up for failure. If you get nothing but resistance despite your attempts to improve the brief, look for and lock in on any part of it that makes sense to you. It could be that the client has wedged a lot of crap into it, and the agency can't get it approved in a more intelligent or streamlined guise.

Even the most convoluted briefs can yield mineable nuggets. It's part of your job to find the actionable and most meaningful part of the brief and to bring it to life in an interesting way. That means trusting your intuition and instinct. No brief is 100% perfect, any more than an idea is.

Always read briefs carefully, but trust your gut. The brief is your partner. You can fight it the whole time, or you can roll up your sleeves and dig into it for a truth that triggers inspiration. If advertising was easy, everyone would be doing it. It's a discipline. Do the work and turn over the stones. Inspiration will kick in.

KEEP YOUR CLIENT POINTED IN THE RIGHT DIRECTION.

Reviewing the brief with your client prior to presenting creative, particularly if it's been a while since the brief was signed off on, is smart. Clients can have frighteningly short attention spans.

Think of it this way. You're coming into the meeting cold. Going through the brief is like deicing the runway for take-off. Chances are, your account person or planner worked hard on the brief. They deserve their moment to quickly walk the client back through the foundational thinking. At the very least, it provides a flight plan and reorients everyone involved as to where you're going and why you're going there. Not all clients are good at this. On occasion, I've seen clients claim they never signed off on the brief. That's never a good omen. Your client may be an uncomfortable flier. Hunker down, and fasten your seatbelt. There could be turbulence.

In the end, how you treat the brief can make a big difference. It's your chance to look like a rock star, instead of an idiot with underwear on your head.

It's Storytime.

The brief had a credibility issue. It said so itself

A few years ago, I took part in a new business pitch for an agency I hadn't worked with before. Their potential client had a remarkable service: they got routine traffic tickets dismissed for the same amount it would cost you to pay the actual ticket. No points against your driver's record. No added charge for keeping your record clean. No kidding.

It all seemed too good to be true.

Working remotely from different cities, my freelance partner and I began comparing notes after we'd been briefed, and realized we'd both circled the same exact point buried deeply within the rather long document.

Consumers didn't believe the client could possibly do what they advertised. We couldn't believe it ourselves. The client had a credibility problem, and it was noted in the brief along with a lot of other information about their fledgling brand.

Their service was hard to fathom and seemed like a cheat or a scam. Ambulance chasers. We felt this was a glaring issue that needed to be addressed. So, we took it upon ourselves to rewrite the brief with an eye towards building immediate trust and credibility among consumers. To help sell it through, I wrote a manifesto that keyed on why the company existed.

The beginning of the manifesto read, "We're for honest people who make honest mistakes." That promise triggered an entire body of work that was empathetic in tone and reminded people of what it meant to be human. We all make mistakes. This company understood that, and had created a solution that helped honest people.

We called the ECD of the agency, confessed to rewriting the brief, and read him the manifesto. He loved it. The agency subsequently pitched and won the business because two freelancers trusted their instincts, and did something they weren't asked to do.

A lot of freelance teams wouldn't consider taking a fresh crack at the brief or creating a manifesto. Neither were asked for in our list of deliverables. My partner and I were glad we did, and so was the agency. Our pitch-winning tagline was, "You have the right to remain ticketless."

The client reported that all the other competing agencies pitched them on humor. Whereas our work chose a different path. Our work made them more human.

We built all our work around the idea of building trust. We took one pillar of the brief and built the entire campaign around it. We didn't ask for permission. We did what we felt was right.

And we were right. Never be afraid to trust your instincts.

Never be afraid to question the brief.

TIPS FOR DISSECTING, REBUILDING, AND UNLEASHING THE INSIGHTS FROM ANY BRIEF.

- A great idea is the ultimate proof of a tight brief. Never be afraid to make someone else's brief better. That's how good becomes great.

- If you challenge a brief, do it respectfully. Somebody spent time on it, even if it isn't 100% right.

- Writing a manifesto before you do any work can rally the people around an actionable insight. And a simple insight can be your key to nailing the work.

- A good planner will help refine the brief, or, at the very least, help you wrap your head around it. Never hesitate to ask about the brief or discuss it with the person who wrote it.

- If anyone takes exception to you modifying a brief, or prioritizing a support point, be willing to demonstrate why you think it's the right thing to do.

- Don't start your thinking until you've digested the entire brief. Let it settle in before you try executing against it.

- Whining about a convoluted brief is easy. Digging into it, and mining a single support point for a great idea is the mark of a real pro.

I'M NOT YOUR MOTHER, AND I CAN'T KEEP YOU FROM HANGING OUT UNDER THE BLEACHERS. **BUT YOU CAN**

Every dumb teen movie known to mankind takes pains to introduce you to the wildly different cliques that exist in high school. The script walks you through each group individually and gives you the crucial drama lowdown. The principal has his or her favorite students, who show up on time, resist cramming freshmen into their lockers, and don't draw giant penises on the bathroom walls.

Cliques are as common in advertising as they are in high school. Replace the cool kids with the creatives, the hall monitors with the account supervisors, the principal with the agency president, and you have the typical agency staff. Yes, advertising people like to break off into packs, huddle like hyenas, and whine like a bad wheel bearing about work, colleagues, and the agency itself.

Many advertising people choose the comfort of cliques over their own career development. Bad move. Try to avoid the pack mentality. Surround yourself with people from all departments, and use your time to sharpen your game rather than dull someone else's.

SMACK TALK. ZERO. PRODUCTIVITY. ONE.

Don't become a bad-habit magnet. While it may seem superficial on the surface, smack talk is corrosive. It's a lot like social smoking. You think you're just innocently dabbling, but the next thing you know you're doing it daily, even hourly. You're suddenly wasting a lot of time in the company of trash-talkers, procrastinators, and malcontents burning bugs and your free time.

Cliques are the daytime soap operas of advertising. Time sucks. Buzz killers. They're toxic and weaken morale. Seek out the company of those who will do you the most good. Those who'd rather study their craft and sharpen their own skills than poke holes in those around them. Mentors and role models. The people who will teach you how to put out fires rather than slinking around lighting them. Align yourself with the right players, and you'll be in a much better position to succeed.

TELL ME SOMETHING I DON'T KNOW.

A lot of otherwise intelligent people make stupid decisions every day. Don't follow them straight off the cliff. It's easy to fall into the wrong crowd and become tainted by malcontents. Before you get indoctrinated in anyone's clique, step back, and consider how those people and their circle are perceived within the workplace. Do you need dead weight pulling you down as you're trying to move up?

Don't get mired down by bullshit or waste your career playing someone else's game. Be selfish with your time. Avoid ruthless politicians and relentless gossip hounds. Align yourself with people you trust and be loyal to them. Be a team player, and support everyone on your team in any way that contributes to your collective success.

Build the island you want to be on. I've written it before and I'll write it again. Shit happens in advertising. It's the natural order. Par for the course. Accounts come and go. Agencies size up and size down. But a solid reputation as a team player with a proven ability to get the job done never loses its luster.

Don't fall in with the wrong crowd. And with that in mind, I'll now stop sounding like your father.

It's Storytime.

"Next year, we'll do it your way."

When I accepted my first creative director job at Saatchi & Saatchi/Los Angeles, I had the benefit of knowing where most of the bodies were buried. I'd freelanced there for eight consecutive months, knew the client, and was treated as a core member of the Toyota SUV and Truck team. I was being included in high-level client meetings. I liked my partner and the head creative honcho, too, and felt I could help elevate the work, which was decent, but far from earth-shattering.

One day a bean counter in finance tabulated my yearly earnings, went to my boss, and flagged me as being a loss center for the agency. Adios, golden goose. The ECD was soon in my office dangling the full-time carrot.

I asked for something I really wanted as a stipulation to joining full-time. I wanted to run the Toyota Motorsports account. It was a calculated ask, and I pointed out the advantages. I'd always had a jones for high-performance vehicles, was already a motorsports fan, and the work at the time was mediocre at best.

I got what I wanted. My creative director partner, Greg Harrison, and I were made Group Creative Directors responsible for trucks, SUVs, and the Toyota Motorsports accounts.

Our first meeting with the motorsports client, Don Ciccone, went well. Like me, he was a gear-head and recognized that my partner Greg Harrison, account executive Eric Coolbaugh, and I shared a genuine passion for racing. We became the three amigos of motorsports, and would soon be giving Don's business the attention it deserved.

Toyota's CART and Formula Atlantic racing efforts were in their awkward early stages, routinely finishing in the back of the pack. If it hadn't been for a stellar off-road racing program helmed by Ivan "Ironman" Stewart, and a wicked ongoing Pikes Peak hill climb team led by Rod Millen, Toyota's entire corporate racing program would have been in the toilet.

Don Ciccone cited NASCAR's work and wanted to adopt a similar formula. Focus on the drivers themselves, as well as the team's owners, and bide our time until the victories started piling up. It made a lot of strategic sense to me, and I left our first meeting determined to embrace Don's vision. Back at the agency, the idea was met with the typical groans and smack talk from the existing motorsports team, who considered his ask to be typical client interference.

Instead of attempting to rally them, Greg and I created a volunteer force from our national group. We recruited people with a passion for motorsports from our internal teams and set them loose on the smaller piece of business. Only one guy from the previous motorsports team asked to be part of the new group. His name was Tom Cleland, an uncharacteristically quiet writer. I soon discovered that he could write his ass off when he showed me some thinking that leveraged Toyota's CART drivers. His work bordered on poetic.

Tom was one of the key guys who stepped up big-time to embrace Don Ciccone's vision. Between Tom, art director Walt Harris, and my AD partner on the business, we were soon hitting on all cylinders, and developing really nice stuff for racing teams who were risking their necks every week to lose. That insight alone pushed the work into a more interesting space.

Our client soon realized we were bringing our A-game every time. He subsequently encouraged us to start showing just one complete, tightly written ad in our initial meetings with him instead of three loose concepts. Doing so allowed us to focus on the strongest ad, and to dial in our executions for the first meeting. It was the most streamlined approval process I've ever experienced and led to the strongest thinking every time.

The motorsports campaign quickly became some of the best stuff being done at Saatchi & Saatchi/Los Angeles. We managed to reinvent the work. Race teams and fans alike requested reprints of the print ads. Don's bosses were even getting compliments from competitors and other sponsors.

Perhaps the crowning achievement of my Toyota Racing Division tenure was receiving a letter from racing legend Dan Gurney's wife. She told us how proud Dan was of the work we were doing for his team and invited us down to his Santa Ana facility for a visit.

That meeting subsequently led to an on-camera interview, in which I spent over an hour talking to one of racing's greatest drivers. We did the same with the other CART and Formula Atlantic team owners. Suddenly, we had more material than we knew what to do with. We cut together spots that intertwined audio from our interviews with footage from races.

Everybody was happy with the work and corporate kicked in more production money the following year at Don Ciccone's insistence.

After wrapping up the first year of motorsports work, a party was thrown for the drivers and their teams at a motorsports-themed restaurant in Costa Mesa to celebrate the season. I got to meet all the racers in one room. It was then I realized that what we'd created was more than a mere branding effort. It was a celebration of people who loved what they did, win or lose. That evening, Don pulled me aside and thanked me, then handed me the keys to year two.

"You did exactly what I asked of you, and made me look great," Don said. "Now I'm ready to return the favor. At the start of next season, I want you and your group to show me exactly what we should do. We'll spend a little more money and do it your way."

The result was a TV campaign that featured fluid, slow-motion footage of cars at 200 miles per hour, making pit stops in extreme slow motion, and narrative that was a mixture of internal dialog, stream-of-consciousness, and beat poetry.

We celebrated the few-and-far-between victories in equally evocative ways. For instance, we celebrated Ivan Stewart's sixteenth win of the Baja 500 with a TV spot featuring grainy, sepia-toned footage shot at ground level, intercut with helicopter shots that captured the feeling of a war zone.

A dispassionate snarl of a voice delivered the copy over imagery. "Six-hundred wild horses, ridden by a madman who eats other men's dreams and backs them with whiskey chasers. Ivan Ironman Stewart, sixteen-time winner of the Baja 500." Even the usually reserved Ivan Stewart loved it. The Toyota Motorsports campaign was one of the best experiences of my career. And I have Don Ciccone and a handpicked team of creatives to thank for it.

I fell in with the right crowd.

TIPS FOR FINDING YOUR TRIBE

- Beware of cliques. Avoid whiners, crybabies, and cynics. Keep their stink off of you.

- Surrounding yourself with people who are willing to work hard and get their hands dirty will pay off, and make you a more capable problem solver.

- Never judge a person by what a clique thinks of them. Judge them on their own merits and abilities. They might just surprise you.

- Foster solid relationships with clients. Invest in knowing them and their brands. Embrace their challenges as your own, and you'll earn their respect.

- If you've ever offered a job on a big account, request to work on a piece of the business that speaks the most loudly to you. The worst they can say is "no," and they might just say the opposite.

- Always be on the lookout for untapped potential in people. If you push opportunity in their direction, you can end up looking really smart for it.

- Give everyone the benefit of the doubt. The underappreciated are often willing to work harder than anyone else in the building when given a real opportunity.

GROUP BRAINSTORMS.
AN UNAVOIDABLE OCCUPATIONAL HAZARD

Every so often, an agency is forced to succumb to the dreaded gangbang, which I'll hereby refer to as group brainstorms in hopes we can finally put the most unsavory term in the advertising to rest once and for all.

That said, it's highly unlikely that group brainstorms will ever be put out to pasture. Most agencies find them indispensable.

Maybe it's a new business pitch. Or, a desperation move designed to salvage an account that's ready to walk. It could be a charade, an unnecessary dog-and-pony show brought about by a nervous account team.

Either way, they can bring out the worst in people.

It's a lot like having to fire someone or dropping a bomb in the agency restroom — awful, but nonetheless unavoidable. In advertising, you're going to be pulled into group brainstorms, whether you like it or not.

But it's possible to get through the process with your dignity intact if you stay on your toes and are aware of what you're walking into.

ALL BRAINSTORMING SESSIONS ARE NOT CREATED EQUAL.

Let's discuss how best to navigate these soul-sucking descents into hell. Consider this an exercise in grabbing your ankles without developing deep emotional scars. The first thing you should do is survey the room and determine how to respond based on who you're in the room with. Here are some hypothetical scenarios to help you put your best foot forward while keeping your other foot from getting stuck in your mouth.

Scenario One–

Do you see your boss? Does he look grim? If so, that likely means that this is the most treacherous situation of all. The client is getting ready to abandon ship, or a recent presentation went belly-up in a big way. Welcome to advertising's Danger Zone. (Cue the Kenny Loggins song.)

There's a lot on the line here, and the potential to tread on delicate toes will be high. Keep your head down, and be one of the chairs in the room. Contribute in a meaningful way, but try not to fall on any swords. This is the Creative Director's chance to save the day and throw a Hail Mary. Don't attempt any late-in-the-game heroics. This is not the best time to throw out the most disruptive idea in the world. It's about threading the damn needle in the midst of a shitstorm without making anyone on the client-side so nervous they get shingles.

Scenario Two–

If the room is full of group heads and senior creatives, this means that there is a serious opportunity at play. The CD has chummed the waters, and the heavy hitters are all gunning to come away with the prize. The political bullshit will be hot and heavy, but if you can ignore it and generate great ideas, you could win the day and walk away with a major feather in your cap.

This version of the group-grope is where I'd advocate the "get in early and try to get a jump on everyone" method. If you're the only one in the war room, take a good, hard look at all the work on the wall. Try to find windows of opportunity in between the existing thoughts. Think fast and get your best thinking up on the wall before the others have returned from the local Starbucks with their first cup of designer coffee.

Scenario Three–

If the group brainstorming session is made up of mid-level and junior teams, it's highly likely it's a just-for-show to make the agency head or account executives believe their lukewarm emergency is netting a response.

Most of the time, there's not a lot of meat on this bone. So, adjust your expectations accordingly. This is a good time to focus on putting ideas on the wall quickly. It's also not a terrible idea to support solutions you see from others, assuming you see anything that stands a chance of putting an end to this little exercise. Think of this as batting practice for the real game.

READ THE ROOM AS CAREFULLY AS THE BRIEF.

If you can properly identify the type of battle you've been dragged into, you stand a better chance of getting through it. Consider the upside. You could avoid a bath in the acid lake, walk away with a huge win under your belt, or be thought of as a team player or perhaps even a savior.

Do your best with the situation you're handed, and know there's glory to be gained even in the worst of circumstances. If there's one thing I can guarantee you, it's that having the biggest idea in the room after everyone has shown their thinking is the second greatest feeling in the world.

Particularly when it's for all the marbles.

And with that, it's Storytime.

How two sophomoric dudes won a women's fashion account using animated sexual innuendos

Years ago, I got tossed into an all-hands-on-deck new business pitch for a retail women's fashion account called "Clothestime" while at Kresser/Craig. The stakes were high. It was a decent sized account and a handful of L.A. agencies were gunning for it. Seeing as our creative department was led by a woman and our department was peppered with a greater than usual percentage of female creatives, my art director partner, Richard Kile, and I had no doubt we were considered unlikely to land the winning idea.

After stumbling around like idiots, we decided to sit in on the focus groups being moderated by our agency's planner, Maureen Craig. We were the only creative team to attend. As we sat behind the one-way mirror, Maureen asked a group of women if they dressed to impress men. One woman made a puzzling comment.

"I don't dress to impress all men. I dress to impress the right kind of men." It made no sense to me whatsoever, but the logic or, more to the point, the lack thereof lodged itself in my noggin. Richard and I put that thought under the microscope the next day, and came up with an attempt to define "the right kind of man."

What if we used whistling cartoon characters and metaphorical cartoon explosions instead of real-life rubbernecking men? We had our agency producer scour stock houses for cartoon clips and soon found ourselves with a wealth of riches. Toy soldiers with their little hearts popping out like a cuckoo clock. Tex Avery Hollywood wolves, whistling as their eyes bugged out. Volcanoes erupting. Speeding freight trains tooting their horns. Animated images culled from the classic cartoons of our youths.

We cut a video together using actual footage of attractive young women wearing Clothestime clothing, punctuated by cartoon reactions. It had no words. Instead, a cool piece of retro big band-style swing music drove the spot for thirty seconds before our proposed tagline appeared onscreen in a retro typeface. "Clothestime. Always in fashion. Never full price."

Even though the animated bits were sexually and metaphorically suggestive, the women in our office swooned when they saw it. The idea became the centerpiece of the agency's pitch, and Kresser/Craig won the Clothestime account. Richard and I managed to beat all the other agencies pitching the account and our colleagues by sitting behind a one-way mirror and trying to make sense of an odd comment.

Go figure.

If you get roped into an all-hands-on-deck concept scrum, never sell the idea of hiding behind a mirror short. Sometimes just being in the room when a curious comment is made is all it takes to trigger an insight. Even if it doesn't make complete sense.

TIPS FOR EFFECTIVE BRAINSTORMING

- All-agency brainstorms can force you into boxes that feel restrictive.
  Get in the box, then challenge yourself to get out of it in the most inventive
  way possible.

- Group brainstorms can be a major opportunity or a complete waste of time.
  Learn to recognize the difference, and apply yourself accordingly.

- Don't get pulled into the typical bitching that comes with wide-open
  brainstorming sessions. Escape from the whining, and get busy finding the solution.

- Never act like the smartest person in the room. Focus on putting the
  best ideas on the wall, whether they're yours or someone else's. Back the best
  horse, and look for ways to contribute to the best thinking.

- Those who walk out of group brainstorm sessions with dignity never show up
  empty-headed or empty-handed. Sometimes they bunt. Sometimes they hit doubles.
  Sometimes they hit it out of the park. They swing the bat. They bring it.

- While rarely enjoyable, focus groups are a great place to find insights.
  Attend the focus groups, listen, and take notes. People win lotteries every day.

- There will always be two kinds of people in group brainstorm sessions.
  Winners and losers. If you're not trying to be one, you're destined to be the other.

REMOVE "I" FROM YOUR **VOCABULARY**

Pick the brains of planners, media people, producers, and account executives, too. Fully leverage their talents. It's amazing how many good insights I've gathered by simply showing a little appreciation for those who perform other tasks that don't necessarily fall under the creative banner.

My radar was always on the lookout for two opposing types of people: those who tried to raise the game of everyone around them, and those who were only in it for themselves. (You can probably guess which type I wanted in my department.)

In today's ad world, the best campaigns are bigger and more ambitious than ever. With technology pushing the envelope of what you can do every day and new media opportunities popping up everywhere, you need a larger and more accomplished team working in unison to execute a truly integrated campaign.

THE BIGGER YOUR ARMY, THE MORE WARS YOU WIN.

I was fortunate. My father always encouraged me to be a collaborator and to include other departments and disciplines wherever and whenever possible. In many ways, he was well ahead of his time. I believe he had an inherent understanding that everyone is creative in some way, and that if you treat them as such, they'll rise to the occasion.

In today's age of integrated campaigns, it's more important than ever to be a team player.

Learn the fine art of the assist. If you focus on helping out the biggest ideas in any way you can, even if you didn't come up with them yourself, you will end up with great work to show for it. Helping those around you succeed helps you succeed. A willingness to share your own great thinking with the entire team can put you on the fast track to a leadership position or salary bumps. People tend to notice people who are unselfish. If your idea becomes something the whole team gets behind, your chances of getting a fully integrated campaign for your portfolio are multiplied exponentially.

Granted, there will still be smaller assignments that need fewer brains. But, more and more the really sexy stuff takes a bigger group to tackle head-on. You can't pull off something like Droga5's Cannes-winning Mailchimp campaign sitting by yourself in a dark corner.

The creatives who thrive in the climate of big, ambitious, multi-channel campaigns are the ones who put their egos aside and make the biggest idea on the wall better in any way they can. Volunteer for the little stuff that might not be considered a big enough opportunity by the "me-first" types. Take someone's great line and write five more versions of it. (Just be sure to credit them in case they're not the kind of collaborator you're striving to be.) Take something from 95% to 100%. Focus on trying to constantly improve the best thinking, no matter where it comes from.

That said, there's no shortage of people who will try to take more than their fair share of credit for a great idea. Some people in this business have built their entire careers on the backs of other people's thinking. If you're a credit hog, it will catch up with you in the end. Because if you fall from the tree, nobody will be around to catch you.

Nobody can do it all. A great collaborator gives credit where it's due. Always acknowledge the contributions of all involved. If the initial idea is yours, put your name on it along with everyone else's. Take credit and give credit. Don't try to claim more than you deserve.

Collaboration is a career skill that can take you a lot further than two people trapped in a room wrestling with a brief. This ironically leads me to two people trapped in a room wrestling with a brief.

CRUNCH TIME, PARTY OF TWO.

Fear not. There will still be times when creatives need to break off into two-person teams. This is yet another opportunity for the savvy collaborator. Even in two-person teams, there's a way to think more productively. If you respect your partner's working style, chances are, they'll respect yours. Sometimes working independently for an hour or two before getting together to compare notes is a valuable exercise.

Getting out of the building to focus as a team can also be a good tactic. Leave the titles at the door. Generate as much good thinking as possible, then curate it, throwing out the derivative and the mediocre. Take only the stuff you think has real merit, but show as much as possible. In a sense, it's a numbers game. The more you show, the better your chances, as long as you're not wasting valuable time presenting filler.

That way, when you and your partner share your ideas once the entire team has reconvened, you're more likely to hit on something that resonates. A direction that you offer up could be the impetus for the big idea everyone throws down on.

Being a pivotal part of a winning team beats the shit out of sitting on the sidelines because you don't play well with others. Think we, not me.

Which brings me – uh, we, um, us – to Storytime.

Bringing peace to the prison yard

Sometimes collaboration starts with something as simple as extending an olive branch.

Case in point, McGarrah Jessee, a small shop looking to move up in stature when I joined them as Executive Creative Director. A cancerous rift existed between the advertising and design departments and was in full swing when I joined; the advertising side felt like they were the idea-rock stars, leaving the design department feeling like a cover band..

The partners asked me to help resolve the rift.

I clearly had some creative bridge-building to do. The head of design was tired and pissed off. I took him to lunch and let him vent. I wanted to understand where all the cross-office ugliness was coming from. He felt the advertising folks were routinely stepping into his group's design projects and taking their best shots on logo assignments, but the advertising group never invited the design department's thinking for print, outdoor, or television.

Frankly, he had a point.

Before I could form a plan, our head of design quit and went to partner in a hip young design firm called Decoder Ring. Rumors were rampant that he was going to pull half of McGarrah Jessee's design team out of the building with him.

Enter David Kampa, an accomplished designer who was more experienced than his predecessor. David had a quiet intensity and a gentleman's demeanor. He'd had his own design firm and clearly knew his stuff.

I was excited to work alongside David Kampa. We were the new guys, and we'd both been to a few rodeos. We had the same problems to solve. I started looking for a way to prove that I was serious about cross-department collaboration.

That opportunity soon revealed itself.

Some friends of mine were starting South Austin Speed Shop and needed to put themselves on the map with a Grand Opening event. It was my first passion project at the agency, and Mark McGarrah and Bryan Jessee agreed to do the work pro bono. Sensing a perfect opportunity to cross-pollinate departments, I offered to work on the assignment with a designer. David volunteered Ryan Rhodes, a young designer to partner with me on the project.

Ryan and I went over to the speed shop and met with the partners. Then we went to lunch. As we talked, Ryan mentioned he owned his own silk-screen setup, and that we could probably screen-print something on rusty metal. Cool thought, for sure. But the shop's owners, who I knew from the local car scene, weren't going into the business to build rusty rat rods.

They wanted to build traditional hot rods and custom cars. That's when it hit me. "What if we printed on vintage upholstery material instead?" Ryan was intrigued. "I've never seen that done. I can give it a try."

While I set about writing the invitation, Ryan designed a grand opening poster which he printed onto glitter vinyl. It worked, and the poster was badass. Silver metallic ink screened over purple glitter vinyl. Within days, we had a couple of dozen glitter-vinyl posters to send out to the speed shop's VIP list. We also had one very happy client. We printed more posters using the same design on thick paper stock and gave them away to everyone who attended the event.

Months after the event, the poster got into the Communication Arts Design Annual. The design department beamed with pride, and the agency partners were thrilled. Not only was it one of the first pieces that McGarrah Jessee ever got into CA, it was proof positive that cross-pollinating was not only possible but worth the effort. Winning is the best medicine.

The healing process had begun. We started having collaboration sessions with all disciplines at the outset of new campaign development. The entire agency began acting as a team. To further inspire collaboration, we moved art directors and copywriters next to designers and sprinkled other disciplines throughout the building. No more silos. We weren't competing against each other anymore. We were competing against the best agencies in the country.

Our recovery would never have begun had it not been for a group that stopped acting like warring factions and started focusing on the only thing that really mattered – the work. The message was clear. We are a team. We work as one. The best ideas win, no matter where they come from. If you can't handle collaboration, get the hell out of McGarrah Jessee.

COLLABORATION TIPS

- A good idea can come from anyone anywhere, media people included. It's never a bad idea to include a media person in the brainstorming sessions. Don't knock it until you've tried it.

- Nobody can do it all these days. Learn to collaborate. If you're not a strong collaborator by nature, take a few cues from those who are.

- Change is the only constant in advertising. If you don't like change, find something else to do for a living.

- Agencies that divide their people into A-teams and B-teams create a breeding ground for poor morale. Share opportunities equally, and many people will surprise you.

- Don't go to battle against your own agency's people. It's silly and nobody wins.

- Taking someone else's idea to the next level is a skill that great creatives possess. Don't kill the improv. Feed it.

- Cross-pollinating between departments can be a highly effective way to break out of the box. Pairing designers with writers, technologists with art directors, and media people with creatives of all disciplines can lead thinking into interesting new territories. Collaboration is not about protecting turf. It's about sharing it.

- Don't sell the ability to collaborate short. It's a major leadership skill and can take you far if you do it well.

STEAL FROM **YOURSELF**

"Good artists borrow," Picasso famously said, "but great artists steal." Allow me to draw an important distinction: Pablo was not trying to make it in advertising.

Stealing the ideas of others is frowned upon in advertising. In fact, there are few easier ways to earn a shitty reputation. And once you've done that, you're pretty much screwed.

Like so many of my peers, I spent the early part of my career admiring the work of Hal Riney and Partners, Wieden+Kennedy, Chiat/Day, Goldsmith/Jeffrey, Fallon McElligott Rice, Goodby Berlin & Silverstein, and a host of other award-winning agencies. To do work like theirs, I studied their work in award annuals with religious fervor. It was an easy mistake to make. Just about every creative I knew did the same.

Advertising can be fun and challenging, but it isn't always fair.

It rewards conceptual kleptomaniacs and honors empty shells. Thieves can get ahead in this business if they're political masterminds. Those who possess more charisma than talent seem to get a free pass. But mark my words, it never lasts.

Admiring award-winning stuff in glossy annuals is fine. Appropriating it for reuse is another matter altogether. That's how rumors get started and reputations get ruined. I've never met a person in this business with a shitty reputation who didn't live up to it. Thievery will make you famous, alright. And once you have that erroneus label, the stench never leaves.

IGNORE AWARD BOOKS AND YOU HAVE A BETTER CHANCE OF GETTING INTO THEM.

I eventually learned paying attention to life outside of the awards books gave me a much wider variety of insights and inspiration. My dad was always a strong supporter of getting creatives out of the creative department and in front of clients, culture, and life itself.

The extraordinary moments that happen in real life and often pass without much fanfare are fertile ground for creativity. Observations and inspirations can be found outside of Cannes, Communication Arts, and the One Show annual. Become a student of everything around you. Books. Museums. Architecture. Film. And, especially, the mundane.

Over 25 years ago, I saw a retail TV commercial I will never forget. It opened on a father joyously pushing a shopping cart through a store accompanied by the classic song "It's the Most Wonderful Time of The Year." Two sad-looking children were in tow. Why was Dad ecstatic while the kids were bummed? Turns out he was piling the shopping cart with back-to-school supplies. Bravo, Staples. I imagine a young parent might have come up with that spot based on a real insight. Not something repurposed from an award book.

An insight found by observing life, and the way parents and kids feel about back-to-school season. In thinking about what it feels like to be a kid whose summer is ending, and, conversely, a parent who will soon be freed.

Point is, there's more to life than studying award books and recycling Saturday Night Live sketches. Studying human nature, taking notes, and pulling from your own experiences as well as the ones of those around you will give you a ton of inspiration. Sometimes a client can help make that happen, too. From my earliest days in the business, my dad encouraged me to go to where the product is, watch it in action, and meet with those who use or engage with it.

Don't look at competitive cookie ads. Eat the damn cookie. Get down on your knees, and look at the world from a kid's POV. Listen to how kids express themselves. Talk to the kids about the cookies. Talk to the moms about cookies. Do your homework. Stop being an advertising person. Be a human being.

Company employees, engineers, and designers have handed me more killer insights than I can count on all my fingers. That isn't stealing. It's being duly rewarded for being smart, inquisitive, and tenacious. For asking good questions until you get a brilliant answer.

With that in mind, I always ask clients if they have letters or emails from satisfied customers or any interesting stories around their products or customers. If they do, I dig into them. They often reflect the company's culture in meaningful ways. As agonizing as it sounds, I've also learned to value focus groups. The experience itself can be tedious, but it often pays off if you listen and take notes. I've derived tons of great insights from people in focus groups, some of which cracked the code and turned into great executions and entire campaign platforms. And the real irony is, most people have no idea when they've hit on a meaningful insight.

That's your job.

INSIGHTS. THEY'RE WHERE PRECIOUS MEDALS COME FROM.

A confession: doing award-winning work stopped being my sole purpose a long time ago. Don't get me wrong, I love winning awards as much as the next creative. But what I like even better is finding actionable insights, and creating work that actually works.

Ask the questions most creatives don't. Take the time to get to know your client and their products on a deeper level, and you'll expose more angles. And the more angles you have, the better your chances are of doing something that's great and relevant to the product.

I've had insights handed to me on silver platters by focus group attendees, engineers, product designers, and clients. On that note, if you can wrangle an audience with a company's CEO, stakeholders, employees, or even its hardcore customer base, jump at the chance.

I've often found that doing so is a front-row ticket to actionable insights.

Sure, it's important to know what's in the award books. But, try distancing yourself from the thinking in them when you're working on an assignment. Recognizing insights from situations all around you will make you a better problem solver and lead to fresher thinking. Fill your cerebral vault with insights from the world around you. Drive to work a different way once in a while. Try a new coffee place. Eat ethnic foods you think you won't like. Make friends with the agency bean-counter, or your neighbor who you've been warned is a total neat freak.

Look at the world from their POV. Become a student of human nature.

Find your insights in the real world.

Years ago, back when dinosaurs roamed the planet, an advertising instructor gave my art director partner and me an assignment for Munsingwear Kangaroo briefs. They were made for men, but I'd never personally owned a pair. My partner, Margie, had never known the pleasure of Munsingwear men's briefs, either. So off to the department store we went to research our assignment.

Once there, we studied the product and the packaging. Like many others, they were white, brief-style, and 100% cotton blend. Similar in price, they had only one point of differentiation: a horizontal pouch design. But, there was no explanation as to what the benefit of such a pouch was or why it mattered.

Just then an older male sales associate wandered over and asked if he could be of assistance. I explained that we were ad students, not a couple of kinky underwear fondlers. He was nice, but obviously knew we weren't likely to buy anything. Before he wandered off, I innocently asked, "Do you have any idea why anyone would want Munsingwear Kangaroo briefs?"

"It's funny you ask," he replied. "I had a left-handed customer come in who swears by them. He says it's easier to get the 'car out of the garage' in Kangaroos." Margie and I were blown away. With one offhand comment, that salesman was able to articulate what the package didn't. He landed smack dab on the "why." I immediately purchased a three-pack. Little did I know that, as a "lefty," I'd been backing the car out of the garage the wrong way for years.

The day to show our ideas soon rolled around. When we presented our findings, the teacher stopped the class to say that we had cracked the code. Our positioning of ambidextrous underwear was a holy grail moment. Victory was ours.

We suddenly realized the value of researching and asking the right questions. Everybody else deferred to Kangaroo gags. Our work, on the other hand, explained a unique selling proposition that no one else had arrived at. Margie and I were the stars of the class. Our instructor did everything short of carrying us around on her shoulders. And I would never be forced to pee wrong-handed again.

That said, it's Storytime.

[I'm now going to break format to share the
following story I read many years ago, as a
young writer, and I've never forgotten it since.
I hope you remember it, too.]

The Capo D'Astro bar
A story written by Bud Robbins

Back in the sixties, I was hired by an ad agency to write copy on the Aeolian Piano Company account. My first assignment was for an ad to be placed in The New York Times for one of their grand pianos. The only background information I received was some previous ads, a few faded close-up shots ... and of course, the due date.

The Account Executive was slightly put out by my request for additional information and his response to my suggestion that I sit down with the client was, "Jesus Christ, are you one of those? Can't you just create something? We're up against a closing date!" I acknowledged his perception that I was one of those, which got us an immediate audience with the head of our agency.

I volunteered that I couldn't even play a piano let alone write about why anyone should spend $5,000 for this piano, especially when they could purchase a Baldwin or Steinway for the same amount. Both allowed the fact they would gladly resign the Aeolian business for either of the others, however, while waiting for that call, suppose we make our deadline.

I persisted and reluctantly, a tour of the Aeolian factory in upstate New York was arranged. I was assured that "we don't do this for all clients" and my knowledge as to the value of company time was greatly reinforced.

The tour of the plant lasted two days and although the care and construction appeared meticulous, $5,000 still seemed to be a lot of money. Just before leaving, I was escorted into the showroom by the National Sales Manager. In an elegant setting sat their piano alongside the comparably priced Steinway and Baldwin.

"They sure do look alike," I commented.

"They sure do. About the only real difference is the shipping weight - ours is heavier."

"Heavier?" I asked. "What makes yours heavier?"

"The Capo d'astro bar."

"What's a Capo d'astro bar?"

"Here, I'll show you. Get down on your knees."

Once under the piano he pointed to a metallic bar fixed across the harp and bearing down on the highest octaves. "It takes 50 years before the harp in the piano warps. That's when the Capo d'astro bar goes to work. It prevents that warping."

I left the National Sales Manager under his piano and dove under the Baldwin to find a tinker toy Capo d'astro bar at best. Same with the Steinway.

"You mean the Capo d'Astro bar really doesn't go to work for 50 years?" I asked.

"Well, there's got to be some reason why the Met uses it," he casually added.

I froze. "Are you telling me that the Metropolitan Opera House in New York City uses this piano?"

"Sure. And their Capo d'Astro bar should be working by now."

Upstate New York looks nothing like the front of the Metropolitan Opera House, where I met the legendary Carmen Risë Stevens. She was now in charge of moving the Metropolitan Opera House to the Lincoln Center.

Ms. Stevens told me, "About the only thing the Met is taking with them is their piano." That quote was the headline of our first ad. The result created a six-year wait between order and delivery.

The moral to Bud Robbins's story is one I've never forgotten since the first time I read this piece decades ago. No matter what the product or service, I promise you, the Capo d'Astro bar is there if you look hard enough. Sometimes it's a physical thing. Other times, it can be a unique brand insight or a function of the media you're working in.

With that, I will now take the wheel back and share a couple of my own Capo d'Astro bar stories.

I found 007 while searching for Chrysler's Capo d'Astro bar

When I headed up Chrysler creative at BBDO in Detroit, I was there for one reason only. It wasn't a love of snow, grey skies, or industrial towns digging their way back to their past glory. I was there to make the work markedly better. It was a tall order. I can honestly say I could not remember seeing a single creatively remarkable ad for any Chrysler product. Other than inventing the minivan, which was no small engineering coup, Chrysler was a brand that really didn't register on my radar.

On the upside, Chrysler was on the verge of launching two extremely interesting vehicles that would take them upscale. I was determined not to squander that opportunity. I asked a lot of questions of the people responsible for the engineering and design of the new vehicles, which were soon to be recipients of Mercedes technology thanks to Chrysler's autocratic new parent company, Daimler-Benz AG.

As part of my self-inflicted brand immersion, I asked to meet with Chrysler's designers and their head of design, a bristly gentleman by the name of Trevor Creed, who reluctantly made time for me. Clearly annoyed, Creed began our exchange by informing me that the marketing department didn't give a rat's ass about design. It appeared I was in for a long, short meeting.

I explained I was new to the account and my group would be launching the Crossfire and Chrysler 300 models. I told Trevor I was truly interested in learning more about the design thinking behind both vehicles. Trevor suddenly realized I was genuinely interested, and he let up on the attitude, albeit just a little.

"Well, what do you need to know?"

"Let's start with the 300. What was the design brief? Who were you hoping to attract?"

Creed explained it was his charge to take the Chrysler brand up-market. That much I already knew. I asked what inspired the 300's design, expecting him to acknowledge the Aston Martin, which was clearly an influence, at least to me. What Trevor Creed said in the next few minutes told me everything I needed to know to do my job well.

"There's no way you could know this, but the 300 had a human prototype at the outset of the design process. It was Sean Connery." Ah, 007, I thought. That's interesting. Then Trevor finished his thought and I had the words I soon repeated verbatim to my department.

"The car was patterned after Sean Connery because you know he could kick your ass, but he's far too elegant to do it."

The Capo d'Astro bar was suddenly right there in front of me. That was the nugget I was looking for. Trevor Creed had no idea how much he'd just helped me. I raced back to the agency and redirected my creatives to take note of the Sean Connery reference as they did their thinking.

That very day, a young writer brought me a brochure headline he'd crafted for the 300's Hemi engine. His headline? "Rekindle your love of the on-ramp."

I felt as if I'd just had my ass elegantly handed to me by six simple words. Trevor Creed would have been as proud of that writer as I was. We were off and running on fertile ground. Ironically, The Chrysler 300's Capo d'Astro bar was revealed to me during a "bonding" session with a guy who thought I was wasting his damn time.

It was well worth wasting.

7-Eleven: Because even stoners need to eat

Art Director, Lou Flores, and I were fortunate enough to work on several different accounts while at GSD&M. One of them was 7-Eleven. The agency was pitching the account, and although the pitch was being led by another GCD team, creatives from throughout the building were encouraged to contribute.

The proposition the agency was executing against was to position 7-Eleven as having crave-worthy foods, which was admittedly a struggle to wrap our heads around as neither Lou nor I had ever craved a 7-Eleven rotisserie taquito. But we were determined to find inspiration. We kept asking ourselves what would ever possess a person to eat such a gnarly little finger food. Looking at the demographic in the brief provided a clue, but we needed to get deeper into the psyche of why someone would crave it.

Finally, it dawned on us. We knew who was seriously likely to eat a taquito from 7-Eleven. A person with a five-spot who wanted to buy a joint and still be able to tame the munchies.

It was an insight we never bothered sharing beyond the walls of the agency. But that simple insight suddenly became a conceptual springboard. I relayed a story to Lou about the stupidest thing I'd ever seen a stoned person do.

I was 17 years old and was sitting on the bank of a river with my friend Dirk and a friend of his I'd only met that day. It was summer vacation, and I had driven to Grants Pass, Oregon to stay for a week. It was the first time I had ever taken a real road trip, and we were savoring our first taste of freedom. There was no one around for miles. We had just smoked a joint which rendered the three of us temporarily incapacitated. As we sat three abreast, Dirk reached over and started scratching around a scab on what he thought was his own knee.

Dirk's stoned friend asked a logical question. "Dirk, why are you touching my knee?"

"Oh, sorry, dude. I thought that was my knee."

No sooner had I shared that story, Lou blurted out, "I once pitched a spot where a guy in a donut shop licked fifteen fingers, five of them belonging to another guy. The client didn't buy it."

Bingo.

We shotgun married the two scenarios, and the rest is history. Our 7-Eleven spot, entitled "Finger Lick," managed to swim upstream through the internal and external ranks to get approved and directed by Craig Gillespie.

We won a One Show pencil for the commercial.

Which just proves a point. Sometimes the Capo d'Astro isn't a physical object. It can be something random that happened right before your eyes years ago. Something that made you laugh and hang on to it because it had a pearl of insight within it. Something that might come back to life as two stoners parked in front of a 7-Eleven sharing a rotisserie-prepped taquito in a strangely homoerotic fashion.

TIPS FOR FINDING INSIGHTS

- Be tenacious about finding insights. Getting outside the four walls of your agency in search of them is a good place to start.

- Talk to the clients about their business. They may be able to share insights or at least point you in the direction of those who can.

- Ask to meet with the engineers, founders, anyone who can give you more background about the brand than your marketing client can.

- Read everything you can find about the company and its culture. The brief is only the beginning.

- Become an insight junkie. Politely push past anyone who tries to stop you from learning more about the product or its true audience.

- Look for the irony in the everyday. Borrow from the experiences of those around you. That's not stealing. It's storytelling.

PITCH THE IDEA.
BUT, SELL THEM ON YOU

Presenting well is important for your advertising career. It can mean the difference between being taken to a meeting or left behind at the agency, particularly at the beginning of your ascent. There is no room for empty suits in a presentation. Every chair counts. If you earn a role, you'll be in the room where the decisions are made. To improve your odds of making that cut, present your work better than anyone else. For the record, it's best to let that be someone else's observation, for the sake of all egos involved.

MAKE NO MISTAKE. YOU'RE SELLING YOURSELF.

The ability to present your work with passion and clarity will take your game to the next level. Treat every presentation as an exercise in selling yourself. Don't try to be anyone but yourself, but be the best version of you that you can be.

Meetings matter. They're your chance to show what you're made of. But, they are not for the faint of heart. There will be blood. Ideas will live and die. You need to learn to play it cool, and not be overly emotional, especially if your baby is being presented. A friend once gave me a great tip. If you're tempted to blurt something out in a meeting, write it down first and look at it for a couple of minutes. If it still strikes you as a great point, then share it when the moment is right.

DON'T LET YOUR BABIES DIE YOUNG.

If you're smart, strategic, and tenacious, you can keep your baby alive, even if the client has issues or concerns with your idea. Listen very carefully to feedback. It's not always articulated clearly or in a concrete fashion. Do your best to get to the core of the issue without attempting to resolve it on the spot.

Don't make the mistake of thinking or acting like you're the brightest bulb in the room, or trying to show off by solving strategic concerns in a moment of spontaneity. Even if you can. Be open to suggestions. Listen to all comments and let them soak in. On occasion, your clients can make improvements. Be open to them, but never commit to anything in the moment. Agree to assess all comments and concerns after the meeting.

Not all ideas survive the gauntlet. Nor should they. Knowing when to let go is a valuable skill. Developing a sense of when to dig in and have a healthy debate about a direction, and when to concede, is as important as being able to close the deal. It demonstrates respect for the client and their opinions.

Presenting with confidence and passion is also crucial. After all, if you're not passionate about your thinking, how can you expect anyone else to be?

Believe in your thinking. Be prepared to play connect-the-dots between the brief and your execution.

Which brings me to a pair of presentation stories that shed some light on how to overcome barriers, including how to win a pitch when you haven't got loads of great thinking to share.

It's Storytime times two.

Land Rover: Respect the rules before you violate them

After helping GSD&M beat both Crispin, Porter + Bogusky, and Kirshenbaum Bond + Partners to win the Land Rover account, I was tapped to head up the business with GCD David Crawford as my partner.

While it was a big deal for the agency, in many ways, the client was still small -- at least as far as car accounts go. As part of our compensation agreement with Land Rover, GSD&M was forced to accept a few non-negotiable conditions. One of them was strictly budgetary. We were told in no uncertain terms that we were not allowed to present any TV commercial that would cost over $550K to produce.

It was made clear to us that over-the-top productions would not be considered. Proposing high-end creative executions would be cause for dismissal. We honored that stipulation without fail, vetting every spot we conceived before our client presentations.

Then one day, while working on a Land Rover Discovery TV assignment, Lou Flores and I had an idea of global proportions. We wanted to tell Land Rover's brand story by demonstrating all the remarkable things Discoveries were doing on other continents. The diverse geography alone was a budget buster. What made matters even worse was that we wanted the camera to perform a trick that no car spot had done before. We wanted it to punch out of the ground and make a sweeping arc over a Discovery doing something remarkable, and return into the ground only to appear back out on the other side of the globe where another Discovery was doing something equally remarkable. The camera would repeat the same action over and over again, each time revealing another side of the planet – and yet another use for the infinitely capable SUV.

The voiceover would wait until the final seconds to pay off the visual trip around the world with these simple words: "The Land Rover Discovery. Uniquely equipped no matter what side of the planet you're on."

What Lou and I hit on that day was a simple yet visually dynamic way to pay off Land Rover's newly minted tagline: "Land Rover. The most well-traveled vehicles on earth."

There was only one problem, and it was a monumental one. There was no way we'd be able to pull off the production for half a million dollars. Not a chance. We'd likely need double that to execute it properly. Everybody who saw the idea internally knew it. Pardon my French, but we were in no uncertain terms, screwed. The idea was budgetarily headed for an internal death.

Proving creatives aren't the only ones with good ideas, one of our younger account people made a brilliant comment upon hearing the idea. "We should bring it to the meeting and refuse to show it to them." And that's exactly what we did.

The day of the meeting in Bethesda, Maryland rolled around, and we threw the perfect curve. We announced that "we've brought four TV ideas with us today and we're looking forward to sharing three of them with you." The most senior client present chased the bait. "Wait, what? You're only planning to show us three of the four commercials you brought?"

"Well, there's just no way you could afford the fourth idea within our agreed-upon production parameters. The idea is too big. No worries, though. You can definitely afford any of the other three ideas we brought with us."

Caveat noted, our client was intrigued and insisted on seeing the fourth spot. They loved it instantly. Before they could ask for a ballpark estimate to produce it, we pointed out that the spot could be used anywhere in the world with a simple VO swap.

Suddenly, the first Land Rover of North America commercial to cost north of a million dollars didn't seem like such a bad investment to our client. And it wasn't.

All told, three thirty-second executions and a sixty-second version were produced at a cost of 1.3 million dollars. We set sales records for the Discovery in North America and filled GSD&M's trophy case at the same time. The spot even ended up in the Museum of Modern Art's permanent collection and held the lead-dog position on commercial director Eric Saarinen's showreel for years to follow. Not bad for a commercial that broke one of the client's cardinal rules.

The moral of this story? Some rules are made to be broken. Sometimes they get punched into the ground like cameras next to Land Rovers.

Diesel: "Let's make the meeting the idea"

(The Diesel Shoe Pitch, rated PG-13 for mature situations and nudity)

Shortly after joining Saatchi & Saatchi to oversee Toyota trucks, SUVs, and Motorsports with my pal, Greg Harrison, it was announced the agency had been invited to pitch the Diesel footwear account.

Yes, that Diesel. The coolest fashion brand on the planet.

Diesel had changed the vocabulary of fashion advertising, and they didn't care who they pissed off in the process. Their ads were sexy, cynical, controversial, and conceptual in a way few other fashion ads were.

Their work was fearless.

The brand was now looking to launch footwear for the first time ever, thanks to a licensee in Santa Barbara, California, who was bankrolling the endeavor. That brought the pitch to Los Angeles, where the showdown was between DDB and Saatchi's L.A. offices. The proceedings would be overseen by Diesel's European director of marketing, a retired soccer star who looked like a hipper, younger version of The Who's lead singer, Roger Daltrey. Good work if you can get it. The other client to impress was the investor, who seemed pretty cool.

Diesel had chosen DDB and Saatchi because both agencies were already working with the brand on the other side of the pond, and doing kickass work.

I myself had a score to settle with DDB/Los Angeles.

I'd left there a year before landing at Saatchi with virtually nothing to show for my two-and-a-half years of hard labor. I believed my slump was due to DDB's management team and my ex-Creative Director, who had a propensity for papering the walls with work but never making client recommendations. My boss was the poster boy for client pandering and to make matters worse, always brought in freelancers on anything resembling an opportunity. It was certainly his prerogative, but was equal parts disheartening and demotivating.

At the risk of sounding petty, I really wanted to hand my old boss his ass.

Serendipity smiled upon us when Saatchi's CCO, Joe McDonagh, handed the pitch assignment to Greg Harrison and me, his greenest GCD team. Our group consisted of the misfits and malcontents of the agency, and Joe knew this was the perfect opportunity for one of our oddball teams to shine. One of our guys was a cocky ex-Crispinite, the walking definition of swagger. He was built like a brick shithouse and dressed like a pimp right out of a Diesel campaign.

We felt confident our teams would deliver. When the time came time for our initial creative check-in, Greg and I were thoroughly underwhelmed. We'd burned an entire week and had nothing. Were our guys huffing glue? At one point, Greg and I figured we might actually be the problem, and showed several ideas we'd rejected to Joe, who was expecting great things.

"WHAT THE FUCK, GUYS, REALLY?"

His response was as agonizing as the work we'd shared with him.

Finally, a solid senior team hit on a simple idea we felt was meeting-worthy. Not earth-shattering, but visually compelling, iconic, and surreal. Meanwhile, our other teams, feeling the heat, were swinging harder and missing by even more. Losing sleep. Blowing off their kid's birthday parties. Resenting the shit out of Greg and me for killing their amazing ideas.

It was painful and our teams were pissed off.

After two grueling weeks, we had only one credible idea when what we really needed was two or three, at least. Greg and I realized that if we didn't pull something brilliant out of our asses, we'd surely be handed ours.

Knowing DDB and their shotgun tactics, I was in the early stages of a full-blown panic attack. I'd caught wind that the best freelancers in L.A. were working on the assignment for my ex-boss. He was going to land the business with borrowed talent. Typical.

I could only imagine the wallpapering party DDB was gearing up for. With only a few days to go, Greg and I sat in his office wondering where our next gigs would be after failing miserably on our first big opportunity as creative directors.

That's when Greg blurted out the words I will never forget: "maybe we need to stop trying to outdo Diesel ads and make the meeting a Diesel ad." It was one hell of an idea. We shared it with Joe McDonagh, and his response was legendary. "I'm not even sure what that means. But I love it! Let's do it!"

We had the green light. With no time to lose, Greg and I mapped out a game plan. We gave a list to our creative admin, Melissa Beaumont, who immediately began making calls and pulling favors.

Starting with our building's landlords, she secured a large empty space in the lobby of our building for our warped performance piece. Melissa called an outdoor vendor and secured a painting crew, then a car-prep company we'd given a ton of Toyota business to. "Can you help us lift a custom car into the elevated lobby of our building without destroying the Italian marble steps?"

Their response? "No problem."

Melissa then secured the following items:

• an industrial-sized paper shredder
• a rectangular piece of opaque privacy glass
• a DVD of Walt Disney's Snow White and the Seven Dwarves
• a raunchy skin flick loosely based on the same Disney classic
• two identical big-screen TV monitors
• an industrial Porta-Potty, the kind used on construction sites
• a copy of Diesel founder Renzo Rosso's autobiography, "Fifty"
• a Shakespearean suit in men's large
• a hardback edition of the Kama Sutra with a sexually suggestive cover
• a ridiculously skimpy outfit for our summer intern, Nikki. (We were surely going to hell for this one.)

Fast forward three days. As the client entered Saatchi's building up a series of marble steps, Social Distortion's "Bad Luck" played at an ear-splitting level. Reaching the elevated lobby, they were met by our scantily clad summer intern, Nikki, seated behind the wheel of my customized 1965 Buick Riviera, a lowrider, its sound system blaring.

Nikki was nonchalantly leafing through the Kama Sutra as her freshly painted hot-pink toenails dried. It was a foot fetishist's wet dream. As instructed, Nikki made no eye contact with the client or the pitch team, nor did any other player in our little production.

Stepping into the meeting space, the client was met by a swirl of activity best described as a Fellini film on twelve hits of acid. The entire room had been painted in Diesel red along with their logo on one wall. At the foot of the wall was an army of empty shoes neatly arranged by departments representing Saatchi/L.A.'s size and scope.

Elsewhere in the room, a nervous little man with a bad comb-over was frantically shredding a giant stack of documents. From inside a Porta-Potty stationed some thirty feet away from our presentation area, a Shakespearean voice was reading loudly from Diesel founder Renzo Rosso's book. It lasted the duration of our 90-minute meeting.

Two large side-by-side TV monitors were stationed near the pitch table with a piece of privacy glass placed directly in front of them. Walt Disney's Snow White and the Seven Dwarves played on one screen, while the aforementioned skin flick loosely based on the same plotline played beside it. Yes, there were "little people" with big parts involved.

A mash-up of both films' soundtracks played at low volume as the Shakespearean delivery continued to echo from inside the plastic throne. As the madness unfurled around us, we calmly delivered our pitch straight up the middle, presenting capabilities, media recommendations, and finally our only creative idea.

The moment we stood to present our creative, on cue, our Shakespearean lothario hurled open the Porta-Potty door and stepped out into the room wearing full Victorian garb. Associate creative director Doug Van Andel, holding Renzo's scriptures before him, made a victory lap around the space continuing his impassioned recital while paying no mind to the meeting in progress.

At this point, Diesel's director of marketing completely lost his shit, laughing so hard that tears were streaming down his cheeks. The best part? We hadn't presented the only idea we deemed worthy of the brand. We followed quickly with it, shared a dozen comps, and confidently wrapped up the meeting.

Everyone had hit their marks. It felt like we nailed it.

Diesel's director of marketing called four hours later, following DDB's presentation. He asked us to assemble our staff as they headed back to our agency. Arriving with a magnum of Champagne, Diesel's European brand champion addressed our entire staff in the same space we'd presented in. "DDB showed us a lot of thinking, and we saw one ad campaign that we really liked.

The client then placed his hand to his heart and let the other shoe drop.

"But what you showed is that you actually understand us." He popped the cork and we toasted the new relationship. It was the single greatest presentation I'd ever been in, and, try as I might, that's not likely to change.

The icing on the cake? Not only did we beat my old boss, but we also sold the only direction we pitched.

PRESENTATION TIPS FOR SUCCESSFUL PITCHING

- Always rehearse for any pitch you have. If you're not willing to do so, you have no business presenting.

- Know your material cold. Practice in front of your wife, your friends, a mirror. Time yourself. Be on your game whenever presenting.

- Create cheat notes if necessary. I carry an index card in my pocket with half a dozen words scrawled on it. They're chronological. If I hit a bump, I'll look at my card, find my place, then continue.

- Eye contact is key. Look at everyone in the room on the client-side. Don't present only to the main stakeholders or your own people. Work the room with your eyes. If you see a nod, give that person eye contact.

- Early in my career, I presented to Japanese clients who would close their eyes. They weren't sleeping or bored. They were listening. Understand cultural cues, and don't let those quirks faze you.

- Always be ready to repeat a point if you suspect you haven't been clear or were misunderstood. If you have time, ask if there are any questions, particularly before you pass the baton to someone less capable of speaking on behalf of what you've just shown.

- Don't repeat yourself, or say what the person just before you said. Move the presentation forward at all times. Time is ticking. Stay on point and keep marching forward.

- Learning how to rewind the tape, land the point, and move forward quickly is the mark of a team that works well together. If someone misses a key point, interrupt, land the point, then let the presenter continue. Teamwork wins pitches.

- Every so often, a client will ask a complex question that has no easy answer. Don't bluff. There's nothing wrong with saying, "That's a very good question, and I think it deserves further discussion. Let's address that in the Q&A at the end of the meeting." You've just bought yourself and others on your team time to address the question properly while keeping your presentation on track.

- If a client has a bad habit of sidetracking your presentations, be polite, but resist the temptation to go down the rabbit hole. Refocus your client and return to the task at hand. Stay the course. Always remain on point.

- Be aware of your nervous habits. If I have a retractable ballpoint pen in my hand during a presentation, I will invariably click it in and out without realizing that I'm even doing it. I've learned to bring a pencil or non-retractable writing implement into pitch meetings.

- Everyone is human. People stumble. If you do so, get back up and immediately continue. The ability to bounce back quickly and be fast on your feet can make you someone people want to work with.

- A post-meeting evaluation of the agency's pitch performance is smart, preferably before you know the results. It's never fun calling a person out for mistakes, but it's a guarantee they'll be more diligent in the future.

- Be tenacious about presenting well and don't hesitate to ask for critiques. The more you do it, the better you'll get at it.

- Take the time to understand your clients, their personalities, and their quirks. Know who you're presenting to. It can only help you be better prepared.

- A great pitch can be theater. Figuratively and literally.

OUTDOOR. IT'S SIMPLE IF YOU CAN JUST KEEP IT THAT WAY

To me, there's no better feeling than producing a great outdoor board. It's like perfect shorthand, calling on compositional skills and brevity. A synergy between words and images.

Done well, an outdoor board can make a creative team look smart as hell. Maybe that's why I've always found it to be so much fun. Unlike other forms of media, it doesn't require a ton of pre-production, casting, or directing. Nor does it necessitate a small army to execute.

All it takes is a creative team, a decent brief, and a smart client. But beyond that, I find that the process of concepting outdoor has other practical applications. When asked to generate taglines, I often perform an all-type outdoor exercise because it forces me to keep the language brief, and makes the process more interesting than simply mashing words together. It helps me visualize the answer. Playing in different typefaces is a nice excuse to experiment with different tonalities.

Outdoor is also a great place to work if you get stuck while working in other forms of media. It forces simplicity, which can lead to solutions that can ladder up to digital banners, social posts, even effective print ads.

THE ADVANTAGES OF BEING SIMPLE-MINDED.

The mark of great OOH is simplicity, and a unique visual isn't a bad place to start. That said, some of the greatest outdoor I've ever seen have been all-type, usually due to budget constraints. The Economist has proven itself to be quite proficient at creating a unique voice with razor-sharp wit using nothing but the type and a red field.

As has CitiBank and ABC television, among others. Great writing doesn't always need visuals. Great writing is visual. No matter what kind of outdoor assignment you're tasked with solving, know that outdoor is a chance to show the world that you're a disciplined thinker.

The rule of thumb for outdoor is seven words or less. But, that rule came long before the internet and URLs were ubiquitous. So, if you want to make sure your outdoor board is super readable and will stand out, winnow it down to the fewest elements possible.

To that end, you might give some thought to lobbying for the URL to be left off the board. After all, people already know how to search for a company on the web. Or, maybe use the URL in place of the logo. Think simply. Graphically. Reduce your elements. Don't mince words. You'll stand a much better chance of making something that will stand out.

All that said, in spite of the fact I'm a writer by trade, I've always felt the best outdoor is visual. If it's interesting to look at, it stands a much better chance of being seen and appreciated rather than merely tolerated.

DON'T JUST COLOR INSIDE THE LINES.

Find out if using an extension is possible. A well laid-out extension draws a lot more attention to an outdoor board. Think outside the rectangle. Stacking boards on top of each other, or doing consecutive boards can also be a fun way to play outside of the typical confines, budget permitting. Sometimes placing the board in an amusing context can make it more impactful. A writer friend of mine once sold Nissan an outdoor board that showed a desert-racing edition of a Nissan truck in action. It was positioned alongside the 405 freeway in Los Angeles. The headline? "You're passing what nobody in Baja could." It was a brilliant use of context next to a section of freeway that slowed to a crawl every weekday.

Spectaculars are also well worth considering since they allow you to leverage technology, attach 3D objects, or even use moving objects to create more impact. And, they're typically located in high-visibility locations. What's more, digital outdoor can be used to create fresh messages daily, turning one media buy into multiple messages. If you're crafty about it, you can continue to change the message, creating an ongoing dialogue with consumers.

There are tons of ways to think differently in outdoor media. If you ever have the opportunity to create outdoor for pedestrian traffic, you can throw the traditional rules out the window. You can take liberties with line lengths, and even put entire paragraphs on one board if they're interesting enough.

I once saw a Mini Cooper outdoor board at the entrance to LAX where the traffic always slows to a standstill. Crispin used that to their advantage by posting a billboard with an entire paragraph on it. A great location and great copy made for another great stunt, which was a hallmark of both the agency and the brand at the time. It made you love Mini for doing things their own unique way, and hate Crispin for being so damn good.

Bear in mind you don't even need traditional boards to do great things in the world of outdoor. Projection mapping, murals, and mobile outdoor boards give you the latitude to bend the rules more than ever. Even a single sandwich board can be effective, assuming the idea is a killer.

One of the first great outdoor boards I ever recall seeing was from my dad's agency when I was a kid. It was advertising Western Harness Racing at Hollywood Park. The board featured a jockey in the heat of a race. Only there was no horse. He appeared to be hanging in midair fifty feet off the ground. It was a great retouched photo image that predated Photoshop by three decades and was one of the most mesmerizing visuals I'd ever seen. I never forgot about it. By removing visual information — in this case, the horse — the board ended up being far more graphic than a typical action shot.

I think that single outdoor board began my love affair with the medium. In fact, I used to beg my parents to drive down L.A.'s Sunset Strip when I was a kid just to see all the spectacular outdoor boards and the coolest cars in Los Angeles. I came to regard outdoor and car culture as the perks of being stuck in SoCal traffic. It sure beats the hell out of the horn-honking and single-digit salutes.

Which brings us to Storytime.

Clothestime: Can't go around naked

With an economic recession in full effect, things were looking grim for my Clothestime client. A perfect storm was preparing to take a prodigious dump on my client's holiday season. Mainstream stores were dropping their prices to the same level as Clothestime's discount fashion, applying the same churn and burn philosophy our client had ridden to success. We would soon be competing against the mainstream brands at the same low price points, and our competitors had the cache of quality in their favor.

Clothestime traditionally ran heavy TV and radio during the holidays. Unfortunately, this holiday season all the mainstream brands were taking to the airwaves screaming "fire sale."

My partner, Richard Kile, and I had an audacious idea.

What if, while the mainstream brands acted like hardcore discounters, we countered by acting more like a mainstream brand? What if we turned the tables and did image ads while the big boys focused on fire sales? We met with our head of media to brainstorm about where we could make the most impact.

As it turned out, being in the throes of a recession meant there was a huge inventory of unspoken-for outdoor boards. At the time, outdoor was widely considered a "reminder" medium, and not a standalone medium in its own right.

Our resident media whiz, Dot DiLorenzo, had a thought. What if we spent our entire TV and radio budget on outdoor throughout Southern California? When she reached out to the largest outdoor company on the West Coast, she discovered they were willing to make a sweetheart deal for all the outdoor inventory they had available.

Having sold our client on the idea, Kresser/Craig made a massive outdoor buy, owning roughly 30% of Southern California's outdoor board inventory for a dime on the dollar.

My partner, Richard Kile, designed a simple and elegant outdoor layout using red backgrounds with black bands containing art deco type. The boards read more like fortune cookies than retail messages, especially since we'd convinced the client to forgo their logo in lieu of having their name typographically worked into the lines.

Los Angeles would soon be blanketed in our outdoor boards with no logos. A random sampling of our lines:

• LOVE IS HIGH-MAINTENANCE. CLOTHESTIME.

• KEEP HIM FOCUSED. CLOTHESTIME.

• LIFE IS A GIFT. WRAP YOURSELF WELL. CLOTHESTIME.

• A FLAME NEEDS FUEL. CLOTHESTIME.

• RESIST MUCH. OBEY LITTLE. CLOTHESTIME.

• CAN'T GO AROUND NAKED. CLOTHESTIME.

Having taken our unconventional shot at avoiding a prodigious beating, we fastened our collective seatbelts and prepared for the worst.

It never happened.

All around L.A., people took notice of our outdoor boards. Frankly, it was impossible to ignore. The L.A. Weekly ludicrously accused Clothestime of intentionally using gang colors, and talk radio covered the controversy. The work earned a rave review in Adweek's "What's New Portfolio." Creativity ran a write-up, and Kresser/Craig got one hell of a case study out of it.

By the end of the holiday season, Clothestime's same-store sales were up 24% over the prior season, which was unprecedented, particularly given the fact that we only used outdoor.

Our hunch proved to be right. By acting confident, enigmatic, and sexy, we outdid the mainstream brands who were suddenly screaming "fire sale" and acting desperate. In the process, we managed to prove that outdoor was more than a mere reminder medium by filling our client's cash registers.

A pervasive outdoor campaign single-handedly saved our asses from a colossal holiday beatdown. Is it any wonder I love outdoor?

TIPS FOR CREATING OUTDOOR

- Outdoor is a truly great form of media for getting noticed. By motorists, creative directors, and recruiters alike.

- Be concise. Capture imaginations. Create intrigue. Then let the drivers drive.

- Remember that outdoor is not just a static rectangle. Extensions, spectaculars, teasers, consecutive boards, stacked outdoor boards, and high-foot-traffic boards in pedestrian-heavy locations can push your thinking beyond the once-limited confines of outdoor.

- The movie business has mastered the teaser campaign. Study their tactics, and replicate them for your own clients. Teasers can work well.

- Coming up with solutions for outdoor can make you a better problem solver in many other forms of media. If you can crack outdoor, you can usually ladder your solutions over into equally restrictive mediums.

- If you're ever challenged to write a tagline for a brand, perform a quick all-type outdoor writing exercise. It takes the sheer drudgery out of mashing words together and I can attest to the fact that it works.

- Breaking the seven-words-or-less rule can be a great way to engage pedestrian foot traffic. That's what we did for Shiner Beer at the main entrance to the Austin City Limits. The result won Best of Show at the OBIE Awards.

- Some of the best outdoor in the world doesn't behave like advertising at all. It can be more cryptic and intriguing than typical advertising. People don't talk about ads. They talk about what intrigues them.

YOU ARE A BRAND.
SO, START ACTING LIKE ONE

Over the years, I've met a lot of smart people who've done terrific work on other people's brands, but missed the mark branding themselves. Deciding how you want to be perceived in this business, then living up to that image, is the most important branding assignment you'll ever have. If people can't recall who you are or what you've done, you might as well be one of the chairs in the lobby.

On the other hand, if they'll never forget meeting you that's the kind of brand experience that bodes well for you. So, let's talk about how you can become a respected and highly desirable brand.

THERE'S NO NEED TO REINVENT IF YOU INVENT YOURSELF RIGHT THE FIRST TIME.

In the beginning, your value will be gauged by your portfolio and your ability to execute smart work on real accounts with actual deadlines. High-level creatives are hired as much for their reputations as they are for their work, so it's safe to say that establishing what you stand for is time well spent. I once worked at an agency that had its core values embedded into the floor of their lobby. I personally found that they lacked many of the traits they so publicly laid claim to.

It's easy to read the all latest business books, and purport that you stand for the same lofty principles. It's much harder to live by them.

So, before you tattoo any set of values on your forearm for all the world to see, take a moment to think about who you are, what you aspire to be, and whether you can live up to the billings. My advice is simple: Once you understand why you got into the business and what means most to you, hold fast to those principles, no matter what. If your conscience tells you not to do liquor or political advertising, don't do it.

Don't let advertising walk all over who you are and what you believe in. It's your life and your career. "No" is a word you should learn to use firmly and judiciously.

THE WRONG KIND OF AMBITION. IT'S WORSE THAN NO AMBITION AT ALL.

A cautionary word about ambition. Some of the most ambitious people I've ever met were in such a hurry for a big title and salary that they may have lost sight of everything and everyone around them in order to get there. By the time they achieved their success, they were likely mere shadows of who they once were with burned bridges behind them.

Don't let your ambition get the better of you.

Beware of blind ambition. Take time to develop a well-rounded skill set. Ambition all too often lacks the peripheral vision and hard-won wisdom that allows you to properly assess and respond to situations. Too much ambition can seriously diminish your skillset and severely damage your career.

Having a life beyond the four walls of a cool office is not just advisable, it's crucial to your ability to understand the real world and life's universal truths.

Pay attention to the divorce rates and work habits around you in advertising. There's a life lesson to be learned here. Work smart, but make sure you have a life outside of advertising. Assuming you want a life outside of advertising, which I strongly recommend.

THERE'S A DIFFERENCE BETWEEN BEING WELL-LIKED AND BEING WELL-RESPECTED. OPT FOR THE LATTER.

I once had a fellow creative director pull me aside to tell me I needed to go to more happy hours with the agency's other creative directors. He believed he had an inside track, but his advice had nothing to do with the work. It was pure politics. I completely ignored his counsel, choosing to focus my energies on the work, and having a quality life with my wife and kids in my free time.

If I sacrificed family time, it was for the work, not to glad-hand other creatives. He now has an ex-wife. Me, not so much.

I wouldn't trade the body of work I did at that particular agency for anything. To me, being respected was more important than being the most popular person in the room. Producing kickass work that propelled me and my clients' brands forward was far more important than shaking hands and kissing babies.

GETTING CHEWED UP, SWALLOWED, AND SPAT OUT. IT'S A VICIOUS CYCLE.

Advertising is cyclical. Accounts are in a constant state of flux. And so are jobs. To paraphrase Bart Simpson quoting George Burns on show business, "Advertising is a hideous bitch goddess."

How you cope with the ups and downs of this bitch goddess of a business defines your brand. It's entirely up to you whether you want to be seen as bitter and burned out, or a phoenix who consistently rises from the ashes.

Learn to roll with the punches, and develop a thick skin. Don't believe everything you're told and only listen to half of what you hear. Be the best "you" you're capable of being. Don't get your undies in a twist over the stuff you can't control, like recessions and layoffs.

SHIT HAPPENS. AND IT GETS ON EVERYONE.

No matter what anyone tells you, you're a number. A line item on an agency's ledger. A tool for the job. And no matter how well-liked you may be, everything can change overnight when the numbers get wonky.

Take layoffs, for example. Going through a layoff is equivalent to a marathon root canal, spreading itself over a longer period of time with less anesthetic.

You need to be on your toes if your number is up. Freelancing can be your savior, but it's harder to do if you're new to the business and don't have a lot of experience, or a body of credible produced work that speaks to your abilities.

Having a headhunter you trust, and who likes you and your work, is invaluable. Maintaining contact through thick and thin is smart. Don't just check-in when you're miserable. Keep them apprised of where you're at and what you're doing. Never turn down a chance to have lunch with a headhunter, and be cordial as hell if you do.

The same goes for meeting people who you respect even if you're happy where you're at.

NETWORK. EVEN IF YOU DON'T LIKE DOING IT.

Never lose sight of the fact that the people you work with on a daily basis are a great networking opportunity as well. Stay in touch with the best people you work with even after they move on. A kind word and character reference from someone who already knows and trusts you planted on your behalf can lead to real opportunity.

Make networking part of your brand. It'll come in handy when you need to roll with the punches. Keep your portfolio and resume up to date. Don't get caught with your pants down and your portfolio lagging. Pay attention to the work you've done and the real-world results it's garnered. The further up the food chain you go, the more important the results are. Know how your work impacted your client's business.

Doing award-winning work is only one measure of a creative. Doing work that meets or exceeds the client's objectives is just as important, if not more so as you move up through the ranks.

THE MARK OF A TRUE PROBLEM SOLVER? CREATING WORK THAT ACTUALLY WORKS.

Case studies are just as important to your portfolio as the work itself. Understanding and being able to quantify how the work you've done impacted the client's business and the category can make you more valuable in the eyes of agencies and clients.

Rolling up your shirt sleeves and solving actual business problems is a great way to build respect and advance your career. And it doesn't require you to buy rounds of drinks for people you'd rather not spend your free time around.

Use your time to establish your abilities and become a better problem solver, as opposed to whining about missed opportunities and crappy clients. Commiserating and bitching doesn't solve anything. It wastes time and it fosters negativity. It proliferates mediocrity and harms morale. Don't fan the flames, no matter how good it feels at the time.

Don't waste your precious time whining. Be a great brand.

You can't have part-time integrity

I once saw Mark McGarrah take a stand with a client that made me damn proud to be the agency's ECD. We were working on a set of outdoor banners that would hang in front of Central Market grocery stores. It was a tiny assignment in the big scheme of things.

But, we were following an outdoor look that had won Best of Show at the OBIE Awards the year before. We considered the account a creative showcase. Much like Shiner Beer, Central Market was a small brand that we invested in.

Great work was more important to us than turning a big profit.

Nevertheless, we were having a hard time talking the client out of a banner execution they'd come up with in-house. They wanted the agency to produce it in the same style as our award-winning outdoor boards. We'd served up several alternative options, but the client had fallen in love with a real clunker, and we were running out of time.

Exasperated, I met with Mark to explain we were on the cusp of producing a real groaner that the client was forcing down our throats. I showed Mark the numerous alternatives we had presented. "So, you're sure they won't buy one of these?" Mark asked. "Unfortunately, I'm positive," was my response.

Mark calmly picked up his phone and called our highest-ranking client, who was usually a reasonable collaborator. I witnessed the following exchange:

"Hi Stephen, it's Mark McGarrah. Listen, we've got a problem with the banner line you folks want to put in front of your stores."

Mark listened respectfully as our client argued to keep the headline. Then he responded, "I realize it may seem like we're making a big deal about this, but, to be honest with you, it's not that the line you want to put up is the worst thing in the world. The thing is, it's bad for your brand. And even worse, it's bad for our brand. I'd hate for anyone to think we had anything to do with it."

There was a long pause as the client processed what Mark had just said. He agreed to take their line off the table and look at a fresh round of lines from us the next day. Mark played the integrity card like few other agency principals I'd ever met. He was clearly willing to lose the account over a shitty vinyl banner, and the client now knew it.

That's how an agency lays it on the line to protect its own brand.

Not only did we sell a better line the next day, we never had another phone call like that with the client again. No client lasts forever. But integrity does.

TIPS FOR CREATING A BETTER YOU

- Always be focused on your own brand and improving it in any way possible. Avoid negativity. If you've got nothing nice to say about a person or a situation, keep it to yourself.

- Being respected is more important than being liked. If you can't have both, choose respect.

- Have principles and stick by them. Even if the damn principals of the agency don't. Never drop your integrity for anyone. Believe what you believe, and be willing to have your feet held to the fire for it. Integrity is its own reward.

- The business is cyclical. Shit happens. Be ready to pivot, and make the best of any situation, good or bad. Avoid unnecessary drama. Adapt.

- Don't waste your time complaining about clients. Spend your free time improving your work, updating your portfolio, studying the best work in the industry, and bolstering your skill set.

- Learn how to solve problems and be part of the solution. You'll not only be respected for it, you'll be a better brand because of it.

- Maintain a solid relationship with a headhunter you know and trust. Keep them abreast of what you're doing and where you most want to be. Check-in periodically. Squeaky wheels attract grease.

IT'S POSSIBLE TO SUCCEED IN SPITE OF CLIENTS. **BUT WHY DO IT THE HARD WAY?**

While creative directors might be the ones hiring you, they're not necessarily the most important people in the food chain. They don't make the final call. They don't hold the purse strings. The client is the one who cuts the checks.

With all due respect to creative directors, the client is your ultimate boss. A strong bond with a client based on mutual respect can make you practically bulletproof. Put it this way, your creative director could hate you with the intensity of a thousand suns, but you will still have a job if the client loves you. Of course, the goal is to not have anyone curse the ground you walk on. But, having a client who feels you're invaluable to their brand gives you a real advantage.

YOU AND THE CLIENT, SITTING IN A TREE.

Earn a client's trust, and you'll be in a better position to sell them great work.

Step one is making sure the client realizes you're genuinely interested in their brand. That can be a matter of asking good questions or showing up at the focus groups when most creatives blow them off. Gaining a true understanding of your client's company and culture can help you better understand how to position them.

A lot of creatives consider their clients the enemy. Don't buy into that tired trope. I'm not suggesting that all clients are worthy of blind allegiance. What I am saying is this: concentrating on sharpening your client skills early in your career will make you more valuable to your agency and its clients. Truly understanding your client can put you in the perfect position to sell kickass work.

CLIENT. SAFETY NET. SAME DIFFERENCE.

I had an agency try to move me off a great piece of business because a fellow group creative director got asked off another account for being an asshole in front of his client. It was a panic move on the part of the agency, so I suggested they call my client first, knowing that she would demand that I stay on the business. I stayed put, alright. Some people might call it politics. I call it career management.

Developing formidable client skills, and deftly knowing when, where, and how to deploy them can put you in a position to not only win but create high-profile work.

To illustrate my point, this chapter's Storytime contains a trilogy of client stories.

It's Storytime, times three.

Chrysler: The handshake that started a love affair

In 2003, BBDO needed a brand creative director for Chrysler. I was available, having left GSD&M shortly before Land Rover's global consolidation at Y&R. I was contacted about the gig, but was far from convinced I was the right knucklehead for it.

Frankly, if it had been to run the Dodge or Jeep accounts, which were also parked at BBDO, it would have been more attractive. But Chrysler? Most people didn't understand that Chrysler was even a brand. Unless they grew up riding in a Town & Country minivan, the marque was practically invisible.

I soon discovered that wouldn't be the case much longer. Chrysler was about to unleash two of the most interesting cars they'd ever created, both featuring an infusion of extremely credible Mercedes-Benz technology.

I flew to Detroit for an interview with Bill Morden, the chief creative officer of BBDO Detroit, and also to meet the president of the office, a man they called the Colonel. While I liked them both, I knew the account was an 800 lb. gorilla, much like Toyota had been when I worked for them earlier in my career. I had nothing to lose by being honest.

I explained that I'd never lived in that part of the country before and I certainly wouldn't be coming to Detroit for the weather. Even more to the point, I had no interest in doing boilerplate work. I was told that BBDO had been challenged by the client to step up their game with the new Chrysler model launches, which I would be spearheading.

I returned to Austin more interested than I had been when I left. There were three new vehicles to be launched, including the Chrysler 300 and the Crossfire, both possessing Mercedes technology and great styling. I was intrigued, but still not entirely sold on the idea that I was the right clown for this carnival.

I wasn't saying yes, but I wasn't saying no.

The next step was a lunch meeting between myself, Bill Morden, and my potential client, Tom Marinelli. I was flown back to Detroit just for this meeting. Unfortunately, Bill had to cancel at the last minute, so I wound up having lunch with the client on my own.

It was a godsend.

I arrived, sat down with Tom Marinelli, and told him diplomatically what I'd been told by Bill and the Colonel. I was only interested in coming to Detroit if we could do demonstrably better work. I added that I wanted to meet with the engineers and design teams behind the new vehicles. I made it abundantly clear that I was ready to do a deep dive to help reposition Chrysler. Tom seemed genuinely interested in helping engineer a turnaround for the brand. And, he reiterated that Daimler was expecting it.

With nothing to lose but a job in a winter weather belt working for Germans, I proposed a gentleman's agreement to my potential client.

"So, if I take this job, and do my homework, you'll help me do great work for Chrysler?" Tom's answer was immediate. "I will."

We shook on it, and I negotiated a one-year contract with the agency that included a corporate apartment. (I didn't want to relocate my family until I knew the job was secure, and good work was underway.) The client was excited, and I was, too. What happened next is a story for another chapter. Which brings me to two men dressed as fruit.

Central Market: What two men dressed as fruit taught me about judging people

Central Market is a small chain of specialty grocers owned by H-E-B, a large supermarket chain throughout Texas. What set Central Market apart was that it was a food lover's mecca, filled with unique items not easily found elsewhere, and staffed by knowledgeable foodies willing to share recipes and expertise.

When I joined McGarrah Jessee, the agency had just won the business. The pitch had been grueling, and a lot of thought had gone into it.

As executive creative director, I had carte blanche to run the business, and build out the rest of the campaign per the agency co-owners, Mark and Bryan. So. I added to the work that had already been bought, including a handful of nice print ads and an outdoor campaign. The agency hadn't presented any tagline options or radio scripts.

As luck would have it, it became apparent that radio was an ideal medium to provide support for the kind of seasonal events that were Central Market's bread and butter. Festivals of Chocolate for Valentine's Day. Beer promotions catering to Super Bowl parties. Thrill of the Grill events for spring and summer barbecue enthusiasts.

We also needed a brand radio campaign that alerted listeners to some little-known store policies. For example, Central Market's guests could sample products in the store. If they didn't like what they tried, they didn't have to buy it. There were also free recipes as well as food tastings and seminars to help food lovers expand their palates.

The plan was to create radio in support of special events while running brand spots for the remainder of the schedule. Central Market was not a big media spender. But, we believed they would provide a plum showcase for our agency's creative, design, and broadcast capabilities, giving us a chance to shine beyond Frost Bank, Whataburger, and Shiner Beer, another small account we treated as an investment.

After being given a mini-brand immersion on Central Market and taken through all the work that was green-lighted for production, I was shown some food images shot as a favor by a talented young Austin photographer named Randal Ford. Randal's only stipulation was that he would be compensated for usage if the agency landed the account and used his images. His images consisted of unique foods, shot in limbo. Vegetables that could have passed for alien life forms. Single-serving-sized confections. Octopus. Stuff you don't see in the supermarket, shot simply, but magnificently.

Noticing the images weren't leveraged as heavily as they could be, I set out to work with them. I also decided I would be the one to nail the radio. In my first pass at the radio spots, I attempted a reverential direction that spoke to experimentation, inspired by an approved outdoor board. It wasn't loved.

I took another pass, making it more playful. Still no bueno.

Looking for inspiration, I called Central Market's Director of Marketing, Frank Hamlin, and asked if I could fly up to Dallas to talk to him about the brand, discuss the positioning they'd bought in the pitch, and meet the team. I thought perhaps a little face time would help me get a better handle on the brand. Frank was the only person who stood between the agency and Stephen Butt, a full-blooded member of the H-E-B family, and our ultimate approval layer.

"We can do it early next week, but this week is shot. Stephen and I are rehearsing..."

"Really. What are you rehearsing for?" I asked.

"Well, every year Stephen and I dress up as giant pieces of fruit and address the troops. It's kinda wacky, but everyone seems to get a real kick out of it."

It hit me like a bolt from the blue. They were willing to be wacky. I hadn't turned over that stone. We agreed to a meeting in Dallas the next week, and I went back to the radio with my new clue, determined to crack the code. I imagined a voice equal parts Dr. Seuss and demented food fanatic, name-dropping exotic ingredients like a trail of crumbs for listeners to follow. It was a lot of fun to write and perform in character, but not much like the work that had won the pitch. When I theatrically shared the spots with the agency principals, they not only chuckled, but Bryan Jessee suggested I should be the voice of the campaign if we sold it. I told him we could do much better than my voice.

I would have an opportunity to prove my point.

Three days later in Dallas, I left the client in stitches after going for broke and presenting the spots as if I was dressed up as fruit. I left that meeting with three approved scripts exactly as written. As I began casting for the perfect voice, I had a feeling that the personality of the radio could inform the other work. So, I asked Bryan if he'd mind if I took a fresh cut at the approved outdoor. He got kind of quiet. I could sense I'd overstepped my bounds.

"What's wrong with the outdoor?"

"Well, it's not very visual." I pointed to an approved all-type board with the line, "There are no mistakes. Just new recipes." "I think we could use Randal's food images," I said, "and be more irreverent ... like we're doing with the radio."

Bryan got real quiet in the way Bryan Jessee has been known to. Then he delivered an ultimatum. "You can change the outdoor if you really want to, but you'd better be right." I swallowed hard, realizing I'd just pissed off a partner.

There was no turning back. I called an impromptu meeting and rebriefed the creative teams. Reading them the approved radio, I suggested we take one more hard run at outdoor, using Randal's images and shorter lines with "irreverence" being the tonal shift.

Five days later, I walked into a conference room with my CD/AD partner, James Mikus, and presented seven outdoor boards one at a time to Mark and Bryan, spreading them out on the empty conference room table. The food images were graphic and used extensions to accentuate the images. The lines were short and punchy.

There was one line I felt was a serious contender for the brand's tagline. I saved it for last, with that caveat. It featured a cherimoya, which can be best described as resembling an edible sock puppet.

The line was, "Chew With Your Mind Open."

The partners scanned the work with poker faces, which I soon realized was their standard response to everything. Without breaking the silence, Bryan looked me dead in the eye and nodded his head affirmatively, then Mark pulled out his wallet. He fished a twenty from it and handed it over to Bryan. Then they both left the room.

I turned to James, not knowing quite what to make of their response. James looked relieved. "That went well, dude." I later learned that Mark had a running $20 bet with Bryan that the agency would never do a great outdoor campaign.

The client subsequently approved all seven executions and the proposed tagline, too. We'd found the brand's voice. The agency went on to win their first Best of Show in the campaign category at the OBIE Awards, and Bryan got to keep Mark's twenty.

All I had to do was bet that a couple of clients willing to dress up as fruit were just as willing to let us be wacky with their advertising.

The proof is in the agency's portfolio. And mine.

Wow!: It took eight years to make the CEO cry

One of the most interesting accounts I've worked on was WOW! Cable and Internet. On paper, they were no different from any other cable and Internet provider. But in reality, they were awesome.

You see, WOW! had a secret weapon: a CEO by the name of Colleen Abdoulah.

Colleen was one of those rare individuals who could bring out the best in people. She had cultivated a company culture that was fiercely devoted to doing the right thing, which in this case was being the best damn cable company on the planet.

WOW! is right.

They'd earned the highest satisfaction ratings in the industry. Meeting Colleen was all the proof I needed. There was only one problem. WOW!'s work looked no different than anyone else's.

Despite all the things they'd done better, they'd painted themselves into a corner with direct mail, TV, and a website just as bland, corporate, and impersonal as their competition's.

That would soon change.

I'd been hired as gyro:'s ECD in Denver. Making WOW! stand out from the crowd was my charge from the CCO of the network. After poring over emails and letters from satisfied customers, I knew what had to be done. We overhauled the entire brand using actual employees in a fun, colorful, differentiating way.

The work wasn't revolutionary or earth-shattering. It was human, genuine, and dead right for the brand. It celebrated the uniqueness of the brand's culture, featured real employees, and mixed simple animation and illustration with live-action and still photos to capture WOW!'s unique personality.

When I stood before Colleen and presented an entire campaign loosely patterned on the Southwest Airlines campaign, she was ecstatic. "I've waited eight years for someone to walk in this room and show me the idea you just presented."

I didn't win a Cannes Lion for WOW! that day, or any other day for that matter. What I won was the trust of a great CEO.

TIPS FOR CREATING GOOD WORK AND HAPPY CLIENTS

- Get to know your clients as people. Pay attention to their sensibilities. Know what work they like, both within their category and outside it. It'll provide you with meaningful clues that may not appear on the brief.

- Clients are human beings, too. Be willing to cut clients slack, and they'll likely do the same for you. Learn to listen to their concerns without being defensive. Don't trash talk your client's competitors. Keep it classy, and that's how they'll see you.

- 90% of clients don't care about winning awards. Talk about something of real interest to them, like moving the needle or building a stronger brand.

- Ask the kind of questions other creatives don't think to ask. That doesn't make you a pest. It makes you more interested and informed. Not only can that make all the difference in the eyes of a client, it can lead to insights others haven't thought of.

- Learn to translate your clients' insights into ideas, and give them credit for the inspiration. Chances are your clients will feel more vested in the work, and therefore be more likely to support it.

- Never miss an opportunity to spend time with a client when you're not trying to sell them something. Invite them to lunch. You'll earn points even if they can't go.

- If you ever have a chance to make a handshake agreement with a client about producing quality work, it can put you on the same side of the fence, establish trust, and create momentum.

- Not every assignment is an opportunity to hit a grand slam or win a Lion. Winning the client over by doing the right thing can win you a fan for life.

SOME PEOPLE SHOULD COME WITH **WARNING LABELS**

In a perfect world, people would come right out and tell you if they're raging assholes. Then you'd know how to deal with them in any situation. But the reality is, you never really know someone until you've been in the trenches with them.

Take creative directors, for example. Some creative directors are the nicest people in the world. They'll carry you off the battlefield on their own backs if that's what it takes to keep the dream of doing great work alive. They're the ones who will teach you leadership skills, and will acknowledge the best idea in the room even if it isn't their own.

They're in it to win it, by showing the best work, every time.

And then we have the creative directors on the other side of the tracks. The mental cases. The ones who can't hop on the happy train without making everyone around them miserable.

They may be vastly talented, but their main talent seems to be spreading a shroud of doom over the entire department. I try to give creative directors with questionable management skills the benefit of the doubt. You just never know how they got that way. Maybe they learned how to swim by being flung from a station wagon going over a bridge.

But here's the thing you've got to come to grips with. They are who they are, and they're sure as hell not going to change on account of you.

SOCIOPATHS. YOU CAN'T WORK WITH THEM, YOU CAN'T PRESS THEM THROUGH SAUSAGE GRINDERS AND FEED THEM TO WILD DOGS.

In fairness, difficult people can possess good qualities. Sometimes you have to scratch a little to get to the good in them because it's buried under layers of psychic scar tissue. Gruff, bitchy, short-tempered, or otherwise bristly people tend to keep everyone on their toes by creating a climate of fear. Sometimes, that climate manages to make the work better. But fun it isn't.

Truly difficult people often have an innate willingness to lock horns with anyone, anytime, and they're perpetually willing to go down with the ship over the smallest detail. They'll protect the work as if their life depends on it because, as far as they're concerned, it does. Think about a mama bear whose cubs are being messed with, or a baseball coach who sees a beanball intentionally thrown at his player's head. You don't want to poke a difficult person with a sharp stick.

More often than not, others will have just as many problems with a difficult person as you have. So instead of taking up the personal challenge of trying to fix them, it's generally easier to be patient and let nature take its course.

It may be a simple matter of an eye roll here, or an "I know just how you feel" there, before an HR intervention is deemed necessary. What it often comes down to is a bad melding of insecurity and ego. Some people just can't seem to bridge the two.

Which brings us to Storytime.

Beware of Richards. And by that, I mean Dicks

Perhaps the single most talented creative director I've ever worked for had no talent for managing the troops or interfacing with clients. He was immensely gifted, but his talent was forged of piss, vinegar, and social ineptitude.

I'll call him Richard for the sake of this tale, and modify his name as the story unfolds.

Richard joined the agency I was at with a great deal of fanfare. While our agency was doing some nice work at the time, it was their hope Richard would lead us to the promised land of Cannes Lions and help attract top-tier talent to our rapidly growing regional shop.

That was the dream, anyway.

I was actually excited to see him come aboard. Alas, my enthusiasm proved short-lived.

Richard's art director/CD portfolio wasn't just good. It was insanely great. Unfortunately, the "insanely" soon eclipsed the "great".

I came to find that, unfortunately, Richard had an ulterior motive for joining the agency beyond a fat paycheck and an insistence on flying first-class while the rest of the agency's creative directors flew business-class.

Did I say Richard? Let's make that Dick.

Although Dick had made quite a name for himself as an art director, he was dead set on being known as a writer. In a somewhat baffling move, my agency gave Dick a high-level writer title when he agreed to join the agency.

I would come to regret that decision far more deeply than anyone.

The original plan was for Dick to oversee our beloved airline account, a legacy account that had helped grow a fledgling challenger brand into a world-renowned powerhouse on the wings of a fun-loving personality and a culture that was the envy of the industry.

Having been at the agency for years, the airline was built as much by the agency as it was by its infamous founder.

Dick immediately set about the goal of making our airline account even more of a creative showpiece. Unfortunately, he encountered immediate turbulence when in a major gaffe, Dick told the airline's infamous CEO that he should ditch "A Symbol of Freedom" as the airline's tagline in lieu of "You Are Now Free to Move About the Country" which was already being used as a mnemonic.

Dick didn't have a clue just what he was proposing to bury that day. And the agency had no idea that Richard was planning the spontaneous recommendation.

Now for the real irony. I wholeheartedly believe Richard was 100% right from a communications standpoint. "You are now free to move about the country" was a textbook example of a great end button in broadcast. It beautifully combined an in-flight "ping" sound effect with a double entendre about freedom that embodied the airline's core philosophy, which was to democratize the sky.

Unfortunately, what Dick was proposing the airline ditch was one of the most heralded and long-running positioning lines in the industry.

Dick's attempt to look like the brightest guy in the room crashed on takeoff. The airline's legendary owner didn't like Dick or his brash recommendation. At the CEO's insistence, Dick was immediately removed from his business.

Dick was suddenly on the no-fly list and the agency had a huge dilemma on its hands. They'd just made a high-profile creative hire only to have him ejected from the account he'd been hired to pilot.

In a mad dash to pull up from the nosedive, the powers that be put Richard on the equally high-profile Land Rover account, only this time with a caveat. He was barred from all client meetings to prevent any more supplemental chemistry clashes.

I was the group creative director tasked with carrying the portfolio to the meetings. I soon learned just how hopelessly screwed up Dick's wiring was.

Within weeks, Dick insisted that his name be listed as a co-writer on all of the Land Rover ads I'd personally conceived of, concepted, and wrote along with my art director, Lou Flores. Dick hadn't even sold the ads to the client. That was my job. I was the guy carrying the work to meetings and presenting it at Land Rover's Bethesda, Maryland headquarters while Dick stayed back at the agency under "house arrest".

At least the agency saved on first-class air travel.

To my dismay, Dick intended to establish his writing credentials without actually writing much of anything. Our Land Rover work was entered into the local ADDY Awards early in the award-show season and won Best of Show. To my astonishment, my name was missing from the writer credits. Dick was the only writer listed.

For all of his brilliance, I wasn't willing to let Dick take writing credit for work I'd written every word of. Besides being a putz to work with, he was a prick to work for. Concerned that my credit would "accidentally" drop off the work in major shows, I contacted a lawyer who specialized in intellectual property. After reviewing the situation, he informed me that I had legitimate grounds for a lawsuit. I had him compose a letter to that effect, and arranged a private meeting between a high-level agency leader, myself, and Dick.

Behind closed doors, I calmly stuck to the facts as I explained that my professional reputation was being damaged by having my intellectual property stolen. I then produced my lawyer's letter. I let it be known to both Dick and the future president of the agency that I was prepared to publicly sue Dick, and release the information to industry pubs, if my name was ever "accidentally" left off another Land Rover piece I'd written or concepted.

As you might imagine, Dick flipped out and called me every name in the book during that meeting. The agency higher-up knew I meant business. The next day, an all-agency memo went out announcing an immediate policy change regarding credits for ads sent out to the trades or submitted to award shows. Dick's name never appeared on the writer line of another ad I'd written, which accounted for quite a bit of the agency's Land Rover output.

The Land Rover work went on to win in just about every award show it was entered into.

I may have put my own ass on the line, but it was worth it. I knew I wasn't well-suited for the agency and that Land Rover would soon be leaving, as they'd announced a global consolidation with Y&R that combined Land Rover, Lincoln and Jaguar in a move that saved all three brands a ton of money.

As history is my witness, that decision didn't make the work any better.

As for the lawyer I hired, he ended up being the best three hundred bucks I'd ever spent, and I never mentioned a word about my internal meeting or the letter written on my behalf to another person in the building.

That would have been a Dick move.

TIPS FOR WORKING WITH DIFFICULT PEOPLE

- Don't work for a Dick too early in your career. It can set a bad example of how to conduct yourself in the workplace.

- Do your homework. Ask around. Weigh the pluses and the minuses of working for a Dick carefully. Reputations precede people who are a total handful, and you don't want to get too much of it on you.

- Dicks can be learned from, but never trusted. Aspire to create great work, but don't trash your integrity to achieve it or take more credit than you're due.

- Never underestimate what a Dick is willing to do for the sake of his or her agenda.

- Dicks do have redeeming values. They're typically willing to battle anyone on behalf of the work. While that may serve the work well, it doesn't make them any easier to be around.

- You don't have to befriend a Dick to work for one. It's best to keep your distance when Dicks starts burning bridges. Don't get caught in the backdraft.

- In learning how to interact with others, pick a different role model than a Dick for the sake of your own personal development.

- Don't be a Dick. And, if you have no other choice than to lower yourself to their level, it never hurts to know a good lawyer.

YOU CAN'T WIN 'EM ALL. BUT THERE'S NO LAW AGAINST TRYING

DOES TENACITY REALLY BEAT TALENT? YOU'RE DAMN RIGHT IT DOES.

I soon discovered I had something the other kids didn't, and it had nothing to do with athletic ability. Sheer determination was by far my strongest stroke. A potent mix of strategy and sheer desire enabled me to routinely beat more talented junior players. Being willing to change my game up if that's what it took to win. Adapting to the environment around me. Course-correcting until the wind shifted and was at my back. Then closing the deal.

The same basic story played out in my advertising career. I bested more talented creatives by simply outworking them day in and day out. Around the time most creatives were cutting bait and heading for the bar, I was headed home still thinking about the brief. I would get a good night's sleep so that I could be up at the crack of dawn with fresh thoughts in my head.

Having an advertising agency owner for a father taught me great lessons about this crazy business. But some of the most valuable lessons didn't come from the industry itself. They came from my childhood and a series of psychological beatings I administered on the tennis courts of Southern California.

Everyone in my family played tennis when I was growing up. And, although I rarely play anymore, I learned something important while competing in junior tournaments in and around Southern California: never give up.

I was never the most talented guy at the tournaments my parents frequently drove me to on weekends. Heck, I wasn't even the most talented player in my own family. My younger brother had a natural flair for the game and my older sister was a model of consistency.

My only real advantage was a talent for never giving up.

THE ONLY BAR THAT MATTERS IS THE ONE
YOU SET FOR YOURSELF.

There's a reason why I bring my A-game to
every brief, and why I suggest you do the same.

Whether it's a plum assignment or something
no one else wants to work on, taking pride in
solving problems will take you farther than
dodging the shitty jobs. Pride yourself on
solving any problem that's placed in front of
you. You'll become a better creative for it.

It's a classic win-win when you give it your all
every at-bat. You'll either knock it out of the
park, or you'll turn a turd into the kind of little
jewel no one expected. That's the kind of thing
that gets noticed by colleagues, clients, and
agencies alike.

IS IT JUST MY IMAGINATION, OR DOES THE
SECRET SAUCE HAVE SWEAT IN IT?

I'm going to let you in on a little secret.
Diligence, determination, and not wasting time
bitch-bonding is a surefire formula for success.

I always loved the little fire-drill assignments
others batted back. Instead of blowing them off,
I was often able to be a hero to my bosses and
the clients just by putting in a little more effort.

The trouble with many creatives is they're
so damn fragile. They buy into the myth that
they're special and deserve to be treated as
such. I respectfully disagree. Real talent often
breeds laziness. A lot of times, the bigger the
talent is, the less willing they are to dig in.
They throw in the towel when the going gets
tough. They blame the clients. They swear
the game is rigged. They blame everyone
and anyone but themselves.

I've always loved going up against people who
are vastly talented but fold like origami. And
I have the trophies to prove it. If you're willing
to show up, compete hard, and apply every
ounce of the talent you've got every time out,
winning is not just possible -- it's probable.

Be willing to go five sets. Adapt your game
to the challenges at hand. Beat the brief to
a pulp. Change your game up, if that's what
it takes to win. Never give up on your talent,
even if you possess less of it than the rock
stars who play one set and then leave.

You can't win them all. Nobody does. But
some of my greatest career successes have
happened when I ignored the bitching and
moaning of those around me. In rounds three,
four, or five. After the prima donnas have
packed up their talent and gone home.

Be relentless, even if it makes you unpopular
with the cool kids. Even if it makes the
planners and account people work harder.
Vince Lombardi had a quote you've probably
heard before: "Winners never quit, and
quitters never win."

Vince Lombardi was a total badass. Follow his lead.

COMPROMISE, AND THE 70/30 RULE.

There are times when living to fight another day is the right thing to do. Ironically, sometimes compromising can be the least compromising thing you can do.

Throughout my career, I've always felt that some assignments are just not opportunity-based, no matter how hard you try to make them that. A good creative director should know the difference.

You should, too.

If only for the sake of your sanity, try this little experiment to see what I mean. If you get an assignment that strikes you as too restrictive to knock the ball over the grandstand, try to solve it in twenty minutes. Do three things that are credible, if not wildly creative. Hit three solid doubles, to ensure it doesn't come back. Present them without apologies or excuses. You might be surprised how much time and potential anguish you can save yourself and everyone involved by rapidly solving fire-drill assignments.

Once your work is approved, use the time you just saved yourself to hit a home run on a meatier assignment. I tested this theory while at the helm of Barnhart Communications in Denver.

After seeing how much work was moving through the pipeline, I proposed my "70/30 idea" to the owner of the agency and the account supervisor of our largest client.

We collectively agreed to adopt it.

Thirty percent of our work, we designated fast turns and non-opportunities. We would turn that work around quickly, arriving at solid executions the client wouldn't kick back. Our success rate was astonishing. The client not only felt we were being more responsive, we were able to go deeper on other assignments as a result.

The 70/30 rule quickly allowed everyone to understand which ads were worth falling on the sword for. The best part of our little experiment? We immediately started having more success selling the ads we felt offered real creative opportunities.

Although what I'm advocating here may be counter to what you've been taught, give it a whirl. But, never lose sight of the fact that even a table tent, a koozie, or a grocery bag can be a golden opportunity.

That said, if you can solve fire-drill assignments fast instead of bitching and moaning about them, you'll have more time to focus on the real opportunities.

You might even find that some of the quick solutions you come up with on the fly can be pretty damn good.

The work we produced became consistently better due to the 70/30 rule. Nobody burned out or had to stay up all night to get their work done. The 70/30 rule worked for us, and it can work for you, too.

Sometimes compromising is the most creative thing you can do. Sometimes giving the client what they think they want is not a bad tactic.

Sometimes, it can actually lead to a great campaign.

Which leads us to Storytime.

The Rolling Stone fiasco

GSD&M was on a big, fat, Roy Spence-fueled roll. For those of you unfamiliar with the name, Roy Spence is the "S" in GSD&M. When he was on his game, he could outpitch just about anyone. Roy had a knack for rallying the troops and mesmerizing new business prospects. We didn't call him Reverend Roy for nothing.

Although he wasn't a creative per se, Roy pitched with a level of showmanship, charisma, and conviction that brought some of the best pieces of business in the country into GSD&M. He was the standup act no one wanted to follow, and, in the time that I was there, he seemed to be getting better with every major pitch.

Case in point: Having won the Land Rover business, the agency turned around and bagged the coveted Wenner Media account, which consisted of Us, Men's Journal, and Rolling Stone magazines. Jann Wenner bought into Roy's pitch, and the agency was well on its way, having created campaigns for Wenner's Men's Journal and Us magazines.

Then the agency's attention turned to Jann Wenner's baby, the magazine that started his publishing empire: Rolling Stone. They were facing a monumental challenge. Sales were sucking wind like a pack-a-day smoker running a marathon in stilettos. It seemed as though Rolling Stone had gathered too much moss. While world-renowned, the magazine was having trouble attracting younger readers while trying to keep aging fans in the fold.

On one hand, you had a dwindling base of aging 40+ subscribers. On the other, the coveted younger readers who typically bought RS off the newsstand – if they bought it at all. Most didn't.

The older demo was shrinking, and the younger demo was consuming music differently. Rolling Stone was no longer considered the leading expert on music by either age group. Frankly, they had only themselves to blame. Years before, they'd made the editorial decision to expand their content beyond music to include movie critiques, audio equipment reviews, even fashion. And, they'd always featured left-leaning political essays and investigative exposés from the likes of Tom Wolfe and Hunter S. Thompson. In the meantime, specialty magazines started turning up and gaining prominence as experts on movies, fashion, and politics. Rolling Stone was suddenly playing second fiddle in the very fields they'd expanded their coverage to include.

After a deep dive into the brand, GSD&M proposed the only course correction that seemed to make sense: Shift the focus squarely back to music and attempt to appease both ends of the demographic spectrum without alienating the other. Jann Wenner and his team received the strategy with genuine enthusiasm.

The whole team agreed it was the right thing to do. Unfortunately, turning the idea into smart, effective messaging that catered to both ends of the demographic was proving tricky. The agency was losing round after round of work under the proposed tagline "The Power of Music," and was taking a pounding at the hands of Wenner and his team, including legendary editorial designer, Fred Woodward.

It was Jann's baby, and, after several attempts, the client wasn't seeing anything they liked. In frustration, Jann Wenner announced he was going to bring New York shops in on the creative assignment if GSD&M didn't crack the code in the next meeting.

Them was fightin' words to Reverend Roy.

GSD&M went into full-court press mode. Freelancers were brought in, including ringers who'd previously worked with Rolling Stone as editorial designers. In short, GSD&M was determined not to whiff. I found out about all of this on a flight to present to our Pennzoil client in Houston. Nancy George, who was an account executive on both Pennzoil ancillary brands and the RS account, spilled the beans. I had no idea since the agency was divided into four different creative groups that functioned independently of one another. I asked Nancy what she thought the problem was. "The client hinted that we can use any of their editorial images," she said, "but the creatives think those images are played out."

I damn near blew my complimentary peanuts out my nose when I heard that. I'd been a subscriber for fifteen years at that point. Still am to this day. To me, the photos in Rolling Stone were a treasure trove of great portraiture from the likes of Annie Leibovitz, Mark Seliger, and David LaChapelle.

Nancy happened to have Mark Seliger's coffee table of Rolling Stone portraits in her carry-on bag and passed it to me. As I wrestled with the notion of appeasing two audiences with a strong emphasis on music, a simple idea occurred to me. What if we juxtaposed current and classic rock music genres using lyrics and images? What if those juxtapositions provided a social commentary?

As I thumbed through Seliger's portraits, I came upon an image of Melissa Etheridge. As it happens, I'd just read an article about her in Rolling Stone. In the interview, Etheridge had revealed that she and her same-sex partner had asked David Crosby to donate his sperm so that they could conceive their first child.

He'd obliged. A Crosby, Stills, Nash & Young song suddenly popped into my head: "Teach Your Children Well." I sensed I might be onto something.

The idea quickly led to a couple dozen more before we'd landed in Houston. When I got back to the agency that afternoon, I asked two fellow music lovers at the agency if they'd like to pitch in. By the next morning, account executive, Eric Asche, and copywriter, Bill Bayne, had come back with tons of additional executions using the artist images shot by David LaChapelle, Annie Leibovitz, and Mark Seliger. And the best part? Their ideas were inspired by their playlists and were completely different from my own.

Juxtaposing lyrics and images was a conceptually fun and graphically simple way to marry the two demographics while beautifully leveraging iconic images from the pages of Rolling Stone. I asked my GCD partner, David Crawford if he'd design a layout that mirrored Fred Woodward's editorial style. It took David all of ten minutes. By the end of that day, we had dozens of layouts that played off the idea. I slightly tweaked the working tagline to my liking. "The Power of Music" became "Rolling Stone. Music Is Powerful Stuff."

GSD&M left for New York loaded for bear two days later. Out of the seven campaigns taken, mine was the second one presented by the group creative directors running the account. The remaining five campaigns never made it out of the bag. I was at the agency tending to my clients and their assignments when my phone rang and I answered.

"Hello, is this Cameron Day?"

"Yes, it is," I replied.

The voice continued. "I just wanted to call and say thank you ... "

"For what?" I asked.

"For 'getting it.' I also wanted to say congratulations. You're now the creative director of Rolling Stone magazine."

CLICK.

I'd just had a very brief exchange with Jann Wenner. I was dumbfounded. Jann Wenner and Fred Woodward flipped over the lyrical premise.

They didn't need to see anything else. It was game over. Hail Mary. Touchdown. Proving that imitation is the truest form of flattery, Woodward had just one request. "Please don't mess with the art direction." As you can imagine, the creative directors in the room were mortified when Jann Wenner asked who was responsible for the idea, and Nancy George credited me as the idea's originator. What happened next was like winning a small lottery. Sure, I still had to go to work every day. But I was now the creative director of both Land Rover and Rolling Stone magazine.

There were a lot of egos bruised that day after Jann Wenner asked to have me installed as the CD on Rolling Stone. Things were a little tense back at the agency, and Roy Spence didn't help matters much when he sent out an all-agency memo announcing that "one of our own, Cameron Day, was responsible for saving the Rolling Stone biz." Let's just say that nobody was feeling particularly sorry for me that week.

Granted, none of this would have happened if I hadn't been willing to step into a powder keg situation and put in some effort. The client had thrown what I felt was a legitimate softball to the agency creatives and nobody was swinging at their pitch.

It all goes to prove that it never hurts to listen to what your clients are asking for. Rolling Stone's editorial photography, in this particular case, was a treasure trove and lent itself to gobs of different executions. The idea was so embarrassingly simple that even a 6'5" man-ape, an account guy, and a younger writer with an encyclopedic love of Southern music could come up with numerous executions in just one night.

Which is pretty much what we did.

[NOTE: The Rolling Stone print campaign I refer to can be seen in the "Work" section of my website at iamcameronday.com. Writer, Bill Bayne, and account executive, Eric Asche, added to the musical mix.]

TIPS FOR THE TENACIOUS

- Be willing to lend a hand, even if an assignment isn't technically yours in the first place. You might end up saving the day.

- Don't worry about other people's egos if you're up against them on an assignment. They'll survive being beaten. And if they don't, it's their problem, not yours.

- Never let politics get in the way of a good idea. Support the best work on the wall, regardless of who or where it came from. Being a class act is well worth the effort, and will help you establish an admirable reputation.

- There are times when it's futile to keep swinging for the fences. Sometimes just getting a man on base counts as major forward progress.

- After a disastrous meeting, a lot of creatives tend to back away from an assignment or give up completely. If you can be the type that continues to run towards the fire, you'll earn a ton of respect.

- Learn to lose with grace, and to win with humility. If you get into the end zone after a game-winning play, act like you've been there before.

- Be tenacious. Even if you don't win, you'll be known as a person who never stops trying. And that's a person everyone appreciates.

AWARDS AREN'T IMPORTANT. UNLESS, **YOU AREN'T WINNING ANY**

Advertising award shows were invented to bring out the very best in advertising and the people who create it. And, for the most part, they do. By rewarding fresh and innovative thinking, the most talented people raise the bar for the entire industry.

These days, if you consistently get into major award shows and are noticed by the right publications, you'll see an uptick in job offers and salary bumps. If you pull off major wins like Gold or Titanium Lions at Cannes, you can pretty much write your ticket unless you're a total parasite.

Big awards equal big credibility.

But there's an unfortunate dark side to award shows. They can lead to award lust, a condition that can plague otherwise reasonable people. It usually preys upon insecure and vain people. And, unfortunately, it brings out the worst in them.

Some folks wrap their entire self-worth around whether or not they get into award shows every year, as opposed to living fulfilled lives.

Sad to say, but you'll witness pettiness, jealousy, and outright thievery in the relentless pursuit of awards. For a handful of sociopaths, award lust casts a wide net that knows no bounds. Beware. Don't let award lust happen to you. You will end up with a reputation as tarnished as those old awards in your den that no normal human being gives a rip about.

As you've likely surmised by now, I'm going to suggest the goal should be to win your share of awards without losing all sense of humanity and fair play. If you have talent, you can win on all fronts. I've walked that fine line myself, and managed to avoid falling into the abyss. Sure, I've won my share of awards. But I don't live and die by them.

THE CARE AND FEEDING OF A HEALTHY EGO.

Over the years, I've won One Show pencils, multiple OBIE Awards for outdoor, and Best of Shows in the National ADDYs. I even had a Land Rover TV spot I conceived and produced included in MOMA's permanent collection.

Awards definitely raised my profile, but they didn't define me. I stuffed the awards on a shelf and focused on earning the trust of my clients and colleagues.

Now it's your turn to do the same.

If you're just starting out, get to know all the award shows and when they take place. Know which ones carry the most weight, and do some tactical planning.

If you're a manager, establish your award-show budget at the beginning of the year, and use it judiciously. Bear in mind that smaller shows are less prestigious. Some are merely glorified trophy shops with no real purpose other than stroking your precious ego.

While winning Lions at Cannes is a huge accomplishment, the entry fees are ridiculously expensive. That's why Lions tend to be coveted by big agency networks that can better absorb the cost and tout their wins on a global scale.

To give you an idea of the sheer amount of money thrown at entering Cannes, in 2016 the Publicis network announced they would not be entering Cannes in order to improve profitability. I have no doubt that it simply no longer made sense to play a game of whose award cases were bigger.

I've never won a Cannes Lion myself. But I have lost in the poster category and watched $1,200 of my agency's award show budget disappear in one fell swoop. My ego survived. I only wish we had thrown a bowling party with the dough or sent an underprivileged child to summer camp with the money. Live and learn.

If you're at an agency that understands the value of winning awards, make sure you're on a first-name basis with whoever enters the work. At the risk of sounding paranoid, it never hurts to take a peek at submissions before they're sent out to check all the credits. You'd be amazed by how many people get left off the credits, or conveniently included when it's feeding time in the tank.

Make absolutely sure that everyone involved is appropriately listed. No apology will adequately erase the damage done if you leave people's names off work they contributed to.

Always give fair credit where it's due.

ENTHUSIASM CAN BE A HIGHLY EFFECTIVE WEAPON.

If your agency doesn't enter awards shows, use your powers of persuasion to make upper management see the light. Who knows, maybe they didn't create enough good work to make it worthwhile before you came along. Approach the powers that be at your agency and make the case, but don't come at it like a glory hog.

Pitch it to the principals as something that serves the agency first and foremost. Convince them it's a way to demonstrate pride in both their clients and the work they do on behalf of them. Point out that it can be a recruiting tool to draw stronger talent to the agency. Impress upon them that it builds creative morale, and justifies hard work in the eyes of staffers.

If you simply can't persuade them of the merit of entering awards shows, it ultimately says something about them and their value system. They don't consider advertising a craft. You might as well be working in a widget factory. You're nothing more than an assembly line worker to them. It may be time to find a shop that values you and takes pride in doing industry-leading work.

AS WITH MANY FORMS OF PLEASURE, SOMETIMES YOU JUST HAVE TO DO IT YOURSELF.

Your last resort is to bite the bullet and pay to enter your work. Yes, it sucks and can be expensive. But think of it as your own recruiting effort. If your work wins, you might be able to appeal to your agency principals to reimburse you and treat it as proof of concept that entering the shows is a good idea.

If your employer is smart, they'll see that you're ambitious and believe in your work. They'll also realize that, if they're interested in keeping you, they'll need to become a believer. Any agency worth a shit has awards, if only as proof to current clients and new prospects that their work is valued within the industry.

If you approach awards in a healthy and balanced way, they can advance your career, and improve your standing within the halls of your agency. Just try like hell not to fall in love with awards. Remember the reputation they help you establish is more important than the shiny objects themselves.

And with that, it's on to another shiny
chapter of Storytime.

A Democracy of mediocrity

When I joined GSD&M, the agency was on a tear. They were already a legitimate regional force to be reckoned with. In my interview with Roy Spence, he made it abundantly clear he was on a mission to make his agency much more than just that.

Roy wanted to be a world-renowned agency without any caveat, disclaimer, or asterisk. A major player. And the fact the agency was recruiting people from all over the country was the proof in the proverbial pudding. They were already big when I arrived, with over 500 people in the building. But in other ways, they were still rather small.

I found that out through our Land Rover campaign.

There were some bruised feelings when my partner, David Crawford, and I were chosen to spearhead the Land Rover pitch. As I later discovered, a lot of tenured GCDs who'd toiled at the agency for years felt they had the right to manage the best brands in the building.

In the case of Land Rover, very few creative directors had helmed a national car account. My experience as a GCD on Toyota's national account combined with a genuine interest in cars made me a logical choice to help pitch and maintain a car account. Partnering me with a seasoned GSD&M veteran like David Crawford made absolute sense from a cultural standpoint.

I brought my category experience to the pitch. Once we won, no one could question that my partner David Crawford and I were the right GCD partners to run the business. Or, so I thought.

After having the account for a year and producing some nice stuff, it was time to enter the Land Rover work in award shows. Having no presiding executive creative director to make the call, it was announced that the agency was going to perform an internal audit of all the creative work to determine what would move forward and be entered into award shows. The agency came up with an internal voting process where every creative director in the building was allowed to vote for the work they felt was award-worthy.

The results were disastrous. GSD&M's tenured creative directors were demonstrating loud and clear that they weren't happy about all the interlopers who'd suddenly come to town, and were amassing a body of work consistent with what they'd done at some of the best agencies in the country.

I'd be damned if I was going to let petty internal politics squander our opportunity to put our Land Rover work in the national spotlight. I let it be known I would be spending my own money to enter the work. Fortunately, reason prevailed when Roy Spence caught wind of the results of the agency's in-house award show. He made an executive call and overruled the results of the makeshift internal award show. In no time, all of the Land Rover work was entered and soon began filling the agency's trophy cases.

The Land Rover work got into a lot of award shows. Perhaps more importantly, the agency never saw fit to conduct another internal audit to determine what should and shouldn't be entered into award shows.

Chalk one up for progress.

TIPS ON AWARD SHOWS

- Award shows can put you on the map, and get your name in front of the good agencies who are looking to hire. So make sure your best work is entered, even if you're the one who has to enter it.

- Befriending the person responsible for award show entries at the agency is a smart move. If that person doesn't exist, volunteer to be that person.

- If you're paying to enter your own work, ask others to kick in. When work wins awards, everybody prospers. Share the credit and the cost.

- Pitch your case about entering work in the most prestigious shows to your agency's stakeholders. Position it as a great recruiting tool, and a way of attracting both higher-quality clients and creatives.

- Always make sure you share the credit for the work with all parties involved, including vendors. Failure to do so will brand you as a self-serving putz, and make others wary of working with you in the future.

- A Cannes Lion is great, but it's no Nobel Peace Prize. Keep your ego in check. Try to have a little perspective if you're fortunate enough to win Lions.

- Don't waste your energy entering low-level or obscure award shows. Anyone can call up a trophy shop.

- Collecting trophies can make you look like a pretentious goober. Find a low-profile way of displaying them. Better yet, take them home, and use them as paperweights.

- Be wary of employers who don't enter their best work. They may not know the difference. If that's the case, don't hesitate to step in, and look out for your best interests.

- Don't ever let anyone crowd their way onto your credit line if it's not earned or deserved. Share the credit where it's due; call bullshit when it's not. Be a straight shooter.

WRITER'S BLOCK, BOOZE, AND OTHER **PRODUCTIVITY ASSASSINS**

Here's a bucket of ice-cold water over the head: if you have to depend on any crutch other than your talent to get the job done, you're handicapping your success. Whether it's an excuse like writer's block, pot or liquor, or lazily borrowing ideas from award books, you're deluding yourself.

"Write drunk, edit sober" is a formula for failure.

People who rely on their talent and work ethic are the ones you should emulate. They're the ones who have it figured out and will have long careers and solid reputations. Drunks, druggies, and people who need crutches in the face of pressure are not long for this business, no matter how talented they may be.

So let's examine a few of the ways people undermine their success. Hopefully, you'll choose a healthier, more productive trajectory for your own career.

WRITER'S BLOCK. THE ACHILLES' HEEL OF PRODUCTIVITY.

I am occasionally get asked how I overcome writer's block. My answer is simple: I keep writing. Unless you're a New York Times best-selling author with a novel or two under your belt, let's be honest with each other here. You make ads for a living.

Creatives who feel they're above the business because they have screenplays or novels they'd rather be writing have no business whining about writer's block when it comes to advertising.

Advertising is like plumbing. If you can't push shit through the pipeline in a pinch, you're of little use to anyone. Advertising is a business. It's transactional. You take money from an employer, they take ideas from you.

At its best, advertising is a craft; at its worst, it's a living. I don't know any simpler way of explaining it. So, don't allow yourself to buy into the myth of writer's block.

Keep writing, keep art directing, keep thinking. Even if you fall short of a home run, keep swinging the damn bat. Clearing the fence every time is not always the most appropriate course of action.

As far as I'm concerned, even a marginally talented creative is preferable to one who freezes up when you need them most, or who selfishly swings for the fences when attempting to hit a single is the more appropriate course of action. There's nothing wrong with losing a battle if it increases the odds of winning the war. Sometimes putting the ball in play is a more productive tactic than aiming for the parking lot over the centerfield wall.

POT. FIRST IT CLOUDS THE ROOM. THEN IT CLOUDS YOUR JUDGEMENT.

Let me be clear about this. I do not consider pot to be an evil scourge on society. It has a time and a place. If you're a war vet with PTSD, a cancer patient, or a glaucoma sufferer, it can greatly improve the quality of your life.

Furthermore, if you want to smoke weed in the comfort of your home, I don't give a rip. You're an adult. You should do what makes you happy as long as it doesn't mess up someone else's world. Just don't puff yourself into believing that pot improves the quality of your thinking.

Don't be the person at the agency who thinks being stoned gives you a creative edge. I can't speak for the entire creative universe, but being stoned makes me an instant conceptual dolt. It makes me lose track of time and hampers my ability to stay on brief. You don't want to bet the farm on me when I'm buzzed.

Having worked with more than a few potheads in my day has made me a firm believer in doing my best thinking with a clear head. I don't consider pot to be anything but a vocational crutch. If you use pot to calm your mind or loosen you up when the pressure is on, there are other alternatives. Join a gym. Take up yoga. Meditate during your lunch hour. Go for long walks.

But please don't toke, and then waste my time. Keep your bong, vape pipe, or one-hit wonder at home, and use it on your own time.

NEVER CONVINCE YOURSELF THAT DOING LINES HELPS YOU TO COME UP WITH THEM.

Don't fool yourself into thinking that being buzzed makes you better at solving anything. I've seen more than a few promising creative careers crash and burn because of bad habits that couldn't be curbed. Avoid the booze, weed, or substance abuse at all costs.

IT'S PROBABLY WORTH SUGGESTING THAT YOU KEEP YOUR LIBIDO ON A LEASH, TOO.

Any indiscretion of a sexual nature, whether physical or verbal, is 100% unacceptable and should be avoided at all costs. There is no easier way to destroy a career. Being friends with your employees on a personal level is even a questionable move, let alone having a physical relationship with a coworker.

It's a scenario that never ends well. Mark my words.

Many agencies have policies regarding this, and if they don't, they should. Now maybe that makes me sound like a stick in the mud, but I'll take it.

There are few things worse than watching an office relationship hit the skids. No one wins.

The real victim is the work. Just say no to personal relationships and trysts, or be willing to witness everything you've worked hard to build turn to dust. If you just can't resist entering into a relationship with a fellow worker, I strongly recommend that one of you change jobs immediately.

Having your cake and eating it too is a fool's gambit. It's hard enough to be a boss or a subordinate in a purely subjective business without making it harder by forming intimate friendships and relationships with employees. Keep a safe distance between your personal and professional life or else.

No need to name names here, but some of the most powerful creatives in the country are unemployable because of this very issue. Don't be one of them.

FIND INSPIRATION IN AWARDS BOOKS. BUT DON'T BE A DAMN KLEPTO.

This crutch might be the most insidious of all. Because, for some bizarre reason, it's constantly perpetrated and tolerated.

Shortly after receiving a brief, some creatives will go into a conference room armed with pads, coffee, and as many awards books as they can carry. They'll sit down and start leafing through the hard-earned thinking of others, looking for something they can pilfer and refurbish. Oh sure, they'll tell themselves they're only looking for inspiration. What they're really telling the world is they're not good enough to come up with their own ideas. They're going through the pockets of creatives better than them and robbing them blind.

Truth is, anyone can do this. There's no real talent required, with the possible exception of how creatively you can cover your tracks. I'm not saying to avoid looking at awards books, altogether. I look at them all the time. I just don't do it with an ulterior motive.

It's easier to think of something fresh by starting fresh. Don't study other people's ads. Study the brief you're given. Study the audience and the nature of the media they consume. You'll come up with better answers by leaning into the problem rather than into what already exists in the award books. Plus you won't have to tear out old award show pages in hope no one notices.

THE BEAUTY OF LEANING INTO YOURSELF FOR INSPIRATION.

I write ads for a living. I feed my family by trying to cobble words together in the most interesting way possible. I meet my deadlines and make sure my colleagues can count on me. It's called being a grown-up, and I highly recommend it.

If I do great work, I have only myself or my partner to thank for it. Not pot, not a miraculous recovery from crippling writer's block, not the idea I borrowed from the back of an old Communication Arts Annual. Getting the job done to the best of my abilities using the best of my abilities is a lesson I learned a long time ago from a killer writer who had, shall we say, a less disciplined approach.

Inhale and hold it in. It's Storytime.

The slippery downside of scoring for your boss

When a new Creative Director gets installed above you in an agency, it's not a bad tactic to try and ingratiate yourself in a meaningful way. But you might want to draw the line at acquiring illegal substances for your boss.

Years ago, everyone at my agency was excited about the new executive creative director coming onboard. We'll call him Bud Stone for the sake of this story.

Bud had made a name for himself working as a writer for a great San Francisco agency. His work was poetic and sublime. He'd been hired to be the ECD of a new Los Angeles office to service a high-end car account that a well-regarded Boston-based agency had recently won.

The brand's launch work was audacious. Everyone in the automotive and advertising industry had an opinion about it. It was unusual, thought-provoking, and daring. Some thought it was brilliant. Others thought it was obscure. But perhaps its fatal flaw was that it didn't show the car. Dealers were livid. They wanted to see the car, not rocks and trees. They wanted to hear about features, not high-minded Eastern philosophy.

It was Bud's job to extend the campaign. Given the poetic sensibilities of his work, he seemed to be the ideal man for the new piece of business. Unfortunately, the account got pulled before Bud had a chance to do anything more than buy a house, and move all his belongings from San Francisco.

In a sad twist of fate, Bud never had a chance to demonstrate his skills for the brand. He suddenly needed a job. That's when the agency I was at snapped him up. Word traveled fast that my agency was on a mission to upgrade its work and client roster, and Bud joining as our new head honcho was irrefutable proof.

To say that my new boss came with a pedigree is a massive understatement.

I was young and impressionable, and looking forward to working with a talent of his level. One day, shortly after joining our agency, Bud asked me if I could get ahold of a good joint, and bring it to our agency Xmas party for him. I was only too happy to accomodate Bud's request.

Cut to the party in progress.

My wife and I arrived at the Museum of Flight in Santa Monica. We had only just touched down when my new boss spotted me from across the room. Bud worked his way over to me and asked if I'd brought a "little friend" with me. I told him I had. Bud suggested we meet at the elevator in five minutes and go for a walk around the building. Against her better judgment, my wife reluctantly indulged my brief disappearance, staying in the bar while Bud and I ducked out.

Once outside and around the back of the building, I lit up the joint and handed it to Bud. I felt honored to be smoking weed with a legend. We powered through about half the joint before we headed back up, our heads feeling nice and fuzzy as we rejoined the party in progress. I worked my way back over to my wife and joined in on the small talk.

Moments later, an audible gasp rippled through the room.
When I turned my head in the direction of the commotion, I saw my new executive creative director passed out on the floor near the bar. Lights out. Nobody home.

His wife was hovered over him, slapping his cheeks like a pro.

Bud was dead as a doornail for thirty seconds or so until a cold wet compress brought him back to life. My wife immediately turned her attention to me. She was not pleased, and couldn't help but wonder if I'd just caused my new boss his first major fuck-up at the agency. As it turned out, Bud had taken a decongestant just before the party and had already pounded a couple of stiff martinis and Lord knows what else, before my contribution found its way into his already compromised system.

Bud never uttered a word about the incident to me or anyone else as far as I knew. I had gotten off easy and learned the lesson of a lifetime in exchange.

I soon discovered that Bud's blackout was par for the course in his world. While a phenomenal writer, he was saddled with a devotion to recreational substances and libations, legal or otherwise.

I gained a lot of great writing insights from Bud. But as role models go, he was a liability. His days weren't long for the agency and I could see their point as clearly as my wife's the night I learned my own lesson about enabling a boss.

The first joint I'd ever procured for a boss would be the last joint I ever procured for a boss. I thank my stars that I didn't send him to the morgue learning that lesson.

The moral of this story?

If a boss ever asks you to score for him, just say no. If he asks you to fill his flask, think twice. And, if he asks you to watch his bag for him at an airport, step away from his carry-on immediately. There's probably a poor junior copywriter in a Third World prison somewhere who'd back me up on that.

TIPS FOR KEEPING YOUR REPUTATION INTACT

- If you insist on working when high, don't show your thinking to anyone until you've come down from the buzz. Trust me on this one.

- Creating great work in the harsh light of sobriety is the mark of a pro. Crutches are best left to amateurs.

- Beware of bosses who ask you to cross the line and become their personal enabler. Politely decline, and bow out gracefully. Preserve your reputation.

- Never convince yourself that doing lines is a good way of coming up with them.

- Passing out cold at the agency Xmas party is poor form. Avoid letting your demons humiliate you in public.

- No matter how good you are, know you will be judged as much on your character as you are on your creative ability once you accept a leadership role. Credibility lost is rarely regained.

IF YOU HAVE NO "OFF" SWITCH, **NO ONE CAN STOP YOU**

Thinking isn't always easy. But it's what advertising creatives get paid to do. And, the better you do it, the further you'll go in this business. So, unless you've got a fridge that magically refills itself, do yourself a solid. Work. Whether you feel like it or not. Let procrastination be your antonym. Become a problem-solving machine.

EAT YOUR CO-WORKERS FOR BREAKFAST.

Unlike a lot of creatives, I like to start early. Truth be told, mornings are my competitive edge and have been for decades. While others are shooting the shit, curling designer coffee, or discussing Jimmy Kimmel, I'm already deep into my productivity pocket hammering out some of my best thinking of the day.

Starting early also gives me the rest of the day to stew on my thinking, attend meetings, review work, meet with others, and make the kind of bigger conceptual leaps that can make a good idea a great one. By getting out of the gate quickly, I feel as if I'm ahead of schedule, and everyone else in the creative department is unwittingly playing catch-up. That's the power of a productive morning.

Which leads me to my very favorite part of the day.

EVERY IDEA SHOULD COME WITH A MANDATORY WAITING PERIOD. I CALL IT LUNCH.

Some advertising folks will wolf down a soggy tuna sandwich at their desk, and call it lunch. Not me. I find a lunch break worth taking elsewhere. It lets me experience fresh sensory input and helps me get my shit together for the afternoon push.

Lunch is also my creative pit stop. I think of it as a mandatory waiting period for the morning's thinking. Given we work in a world of constant deadlines, you don't have the luxury of putting an idea in a drawer for weeks. But you can park it for an hour, and sometimes that makes all the difference.

Having a good meal, taking a stroll, hitting the gym, or running an errand during your lunch hour can give you just enough distance to keep you from falling in love with the smell of your own thinking. When you return, be tough on your ideas. Ask yourself if it's too derivative of anything else you've seen. Does it still look like a gem? If so, great. If not, go back to the conceptual salt mines. There's nothing wrong with tossing an idea back if it doesn't serve the brief.

Ideas need time to percolate. People need to eat. And wouldn't you know it, lunch hour occurs every day. Perfect.

I typically carry a notebook to record random thoughts or tend to low-level housekeeping while at lunch. There's no need to panic. The day is unfolding productively and there's plenty of daylight left to throw down more thinking if it's needed.

A PRODUCTIVE THOUGHT: WHY DON'T YOU DICK AROUND ON YOUR OWN DIME?

I try to limit the socializing and shit shooting to my lunch hour. It sets a tone. I'm at work to work. I value my job. I use my time to try and nail good ideas to the wall whether I'm concepting or curating them.

I don't mean to sound like a buzzkill, but I get paid to generate kickass thinking and to help advance the thinking of my fellow creatives, not to play Ping-Pong and share funny cat videos. I don't get paid to practice stand-up or slow other people down and neither do you. I get paid to solve problems and to keep the ball in play. And, at the risk of sounding like your boss, you get paid to do the same.

If you squander your entire day dicking around, that's your choice. But don't slow me down, or handicap your colleagues who want to get home to their families at the end of the day. Learn to get your work done at work while the phones are ringing.

Pulling the night shift to get your shit done is a formula for misery and mental burnout. Too many creatives fall into that cycle, blaming everyone but themselves. Don't fall into that all-too-familiar pattern.

I actively avoid burning up my daylight and letting the fires build under my ass. That's not motivating to me. It's like shoving a stick into your own spokes and blaming others for the bicycle accident. I find the early-bird route a more productive one, and a good fit for how I'm wired.

Given the option, I'll always start early and walk out five minutes after the account guys do, assuming I've got my shit squared away.

You just might find you get a better life out of the deal if you do the same.

NEVER APOLOGIZE FOR KILLING IT ON YOUR OWN TERMS.

Figure out what works for you, and stick by it. If your partner's biological time clock runs counter to yours, find a compromise that works for both of you. Establish a happy medium or divide and conquer.

Working independently of each other, and using your time together to curate your collective thinking might just be the winning formula if you have varying productivity cycles.

You might get a lot more thinking done that way. After all, writers sometimes need to crank on words without interruption, and art directors need time to lay things out or get their own thoughts down in writing.

I've always liked working with art directors who like to write. I find they're generally just as open to writers who think visually. As I see it, that doubles the chances of coming up with something great. When you're tasked with constantly solving marketing problems, two ideators who refuse to allow themselves to be limited by their job titles are better than one. So try dropping those titles, and focusing on big ideas.

That's often the sign of a killer team. Neither partner cares where the idea comes from. They both get behind the best ideas and push like hell. When egos are set aside, and the respect is mutual, the potential for great work expands exponentially.

TO THINE OWN TWISTED WIRING BE TRUE.

Maybe you like to wear a garter belt under your jeans. Maybe you need to pretend that your partner is a Tibetan goat herder. Maybe you do your best work on a public bus at 3 AM.

As a manager, I never gave a rat's ass what my creatives did or where they did it, as long as they delivered the goods and didn't give the agency HR people hives. People respect commitment, even if it comes at the expense of idiosyncrasies. Your colleagues will learn to live with your quirks if you always hold up your end of the bargain.

Be consistent and establish your personal work bubble. Just make sure to let your bosses and account people know you're working on their assignments, particularly if you go off-site. If you're doing a great job, they'll help block for you. There will be exceptions, of course. There are times when you'll have to be in the building. But, it never hurts to have an understanding with the people who depend on you. Oh, and let the creative coordinator know how you can be reached.

Folks might not understand the motivation behind that tinfoil hat of yours. It doesn't matter, as long as you stay out of electrical storms and keep the ideas pouring.

Which is the perfect segue for
another Storytime.

I hired the perfect writer for the job, twice

Personal quirks aren't all that unusual in creative people. Sometimes it's one little thing. Other times, it's a lot of little things. And, on occasion, it's just that a person doesn't fit the cliché of the typical advertising creative.

Case in point, Ricky Lambert.

Ricky was a young writer I hired in Denver. To be more precise, he's a young writer I hired twice in Denver. What makes one writer so desirable that a boss is willing to double down? Ricky was the ideal candidate for the job on both occasions.

When I first interviewed him, I was functioning as both an ECD and a writer at a small agency where every chair counted. We had one big client and a handful of smaller ankle biters. I had a lot of respect for our biggest account – and not just because they were our biggest account. They'd built a great culture and the work we were doing needed to do a better job of reflecting it.

I needed a writer who could help me tell their story, and tell it well. We did a fair share of print, a bit of TV, and a metric shit ton of direct mail.

I didn't have the budget for a middleweight creative or even a headhunter for that matter. But, I was holding out for the right person. I knew I'd be toast if my new writer wasn't talented, a quick study, and interested in capturing the essence of my clients' brands.

One night, I saw a Denver Egotist post written by Mike Sukle, a creative director and a principal of a fellow Denver agency I'd come to admire. Sukle had been asked to write a year-in-review piece. Among the highlights of his year, he mentioned a young writer he'd brought in as an intern, but didn't have the budget to hire.

I called Mike for the lowdown, and he sent Ricky my way. But first, he advised me, "He's kinda quiet, but he's a good writer." Ricky lived up to both billings. While he was indeed on the quiet end of the spectrum, his work was packed with personality. He had thoughtful stuff, ironic stuff, laugh-out-loud funny stuff.

I told Ricky what the gig would require. The more we talked, the more I became convinced he was the right guy for the job. So, I hit him with my pitch. I told Ricky that we did a lot of print and direct mail and that he'd have to split the workload with me 50-50. In return, I'd let him work with Rob Lewis, a senior art director I'd hired, who I knew would be willing to mentor him.

I promised him the opportunity to work on every project, good or bad. I'd mentor Ricky and help develop other skills such as presenting, directing voice talent, casting commercials, and working with vendors – the whole nine yards.

Ricky accepted the job.

He soon proved to have ninja skills as a writer. He made my job easier and saved us a boatload of time. Rob Lewis and I invested that time back into mentoring him. All Ricky needed was to become more comfortable in those areas where he didn't already excel. Rob and I took Ricky under our wings, coached him through processes, dragged him to meetings, and had him present his work. We functioned as a safety net that he rarely needed.

I took Ricky to radio recording sessions, had him take the reins and direct talent, and shadowed him on TV shoots. I coached him to project when he presented, and to show genuine enthusiasm for his concepts. I treated Ricky like a younger brother and made sure everyone knew that if they messed with him, they'd be messing with me.

Although Ricky didn't say much in the beginning, his work always spoke volumes. His confidence grew as people soon realized just how good he was. In no time, he went from being "the quiet one" to the one everyone wanted to have on their assignments.

Ricky was one of the best entry-level hires I'd ever made.

Consequently, when I left gyro: for Barnhart, I made Ricky the same offer I had before, only at a higher salary, and with more responsibility and opportunity attached. Sometimes, lightning does strike twice.

Ricky Lambert is living proof that big talent can hide in plain sight, within a person who's shy, quiet, and refreshingly modest. I remember having lunch with another creative director in Denver. I told him that I'd hired a young writer who was going to do great things. When I mentioned Ricky's name, the creative director's jaw hit the floor.

"Really? I can't believe you hired that guy! We interviewed him, and he barely talked. I thought he was totally weird. I couldn't see how he'd fit in at my place." I wasn't hiring Ricky to fit in. I was hiring him to stand out. To write great headlines, body copy, social posts, radio, and TV spots. To be dead-on the brief, and care about the details.

I hired Ricky to learn the stuff that could be taught. As far as I was concerned, he already had the sheer writing talent.

When I gave notice at Barnhart and made the decision to return to Austin and freelance life, I wanted Ricky to know I wasn't abandoning him. Believing he'd gone as far as he could at Barnhart, I asked Ricky where he most wanted to work. He told me Cactus, which was a top Denver agency.

I called their ECD, Norm Shearer, whom I'd met at an advertising event, and asked him a favor. "Would you mind looking at the portfolio of a young writer who worked for me? If you like what you see, call me. I'll tell you why you'd be crazy not to hire him."

Ricky started at Cactus a few weeks later.

Three years later, Mike Sukle called Ricky. He was looking for a senior writer to join his agency and immediately called his past intern. I can't say I was surprised. After all, long before either Norm or I had discovered Ricky's talent, Mike had seen it firsthand.

Ricky was now back at what I consider to be one of the best small agencies in the country, working for the guy who originally sent him my way. Sukle got a senior writer. A more comfortable presenter. A dude with a few more rodeos under his belt. A person who was passed over by others because he didn't fit the stereotype of the typical advertising creative.

Mike got a great thinker. But, he already knew that.

TIPS FOR BECOMING RIDICULOUSLY PRODUCTIVE

- Procrastination is a disease that affects far too many creatives. Avoid it.

- Find when and where you do your best work, and spend as much time in that zone as possible.

- There's nothing wrong with being an early bird if you're wired for it. You can use it to your advantage by having meaningful conversations before the craziness kicks in.

- Getting out of the building for lunch can be a very productive thing to do. Walk away from your thinking, and come back to it fresh. You'll be able to evaluate it better.

- Goofing off at the office is no way to waste your day. Learn to get your work done at work, and you'll have more time to play later.

- You're only as good as your work. If you're going to fly your freak flag, you had better be freakin' good.

- Judge people by their character and their thinking, not by whether they fit your preconceived notion of what an advertising creative should look like. Still waters run deep. Sometimes it's the quiet ones who do the best thinking.

- If you ever get the chance to mentor someone grateful for the opportunity, do it. You'll both benefit from the experience.

- Take the time to really read a writer's work. It often says things about them they wouldn't say about themselves.

- Loud people do good work, too. Be authentic, and develop your skills based on who you are. Play to your strengths, and work to improve your weaknesses. Be true to yourself.

- It's been my experience that weird is a good trait, as long as it's attached to responsibility. Weird is different. And different is good.

WITH ANY LUCK, THE RIGHT TOOL FOR THE JOB **WON'T BE ONE**

Let's say you just sold a TV spot or, better yet, a multi-spot campaign. You're excited, and you should be. The client has signed off on your thinking, and you're heading into production.

Now for the bad news.

Some people will try to horn in on a successful idea any way they can. Before you know it, they're guiding the production down a path that has nothing to do with the idea you originally envisioned, or adding their name to your spot when it goes out for award show consideration.

The producer may have made a pay-it-forward deal from the last spot or package he awarded to a specific production company. The creative director may have favors to pay, or production companies he wants to score points with.

So, how do you make sure the needs of your work come first?

MARK YOUR TERRITORY WITHOUT LIFTING YOUR LEG.

First off, claim ownership loudly and proudly. Send out an email thanking everyone, letting them know in subtle but no uncertain terms that the account team and the creative director did a great job helping sell THE SPOT YOU AND YOUR PARTNER CAME UP WITH. You can be subtler than using all caps, but surely you get my drift.

Be involved in every aspect of the production, however seemingly minor. Leave no gaps for others to insert agendas that don't serve your idea. Surround yourself with as much selfless talent as possible and the better off your production will be.

FIND YOUR VERY OWN COPPOLA.

Assemble a director list, and make notes about what the directors you've chosen would bring to the idea. Look at as many reels as possible. Not just the ones the agency producer brings you. If it's your idea, stick to your guns. Consider the most reputable production companies because they didn't get that way by half-assing. They know what they're doing, and typically will not cut corners. Granted, they may not necessarily have the coolest production company T-shirts. They may not need to play that game.

You will be tempted to get the hottest director on the scene at the time. Hot is sexy. But it's usually smarter to look for a director who's the best possible fit. Maybe the hot director from three or four years ago has a lot more experience with your kind of idea. That can come in handy, particularly if you don't have much experience yourself.

Some directors couldn't give a fuck about your idea, your client, or the sanctity of the agency/client relationship. They care only about themselves. So, by all means, pay attention to reputations.

Reputations are usually well-earned and if you hear a director is difficult, ask yourself if that's something you really want. Some high-end directors are tyrants and establish a tense atmosphere as part of their own pathetic power trip.

With that in mind you may be better off considering an up-and-comer. They're often more passionate about producing something great and aren't bankrolling a house in the Hollywood Hills, or operating under the influence of Peruvian marching powder.

They'll generally spend more time on your spot, be a more willing collaborator, and look for ways to plus the project in any way they can. Like you, they're at a point in their career where they're looking for ways to make their work better.

CONSIDER A-LIST DIRECTORS, BUT BE MINDFUL OF WHAT THE "A" STANDS FOR.

There's nothing wrong with picking a few pie-in-the-sky options that could slay on your spot, even if they're outside your budget. You never know when a star might fall in love with your idea, and be willing to find a way to make it work.

Just be mindful that a lot of A-list directors will try to reimagine your script for the sake of their precious egos. Be prepared to call bullshit. They didn't nail the brief. They didn't do the work of selling the damn spot. So, don't let the director unravel it. It's your spot, so make sure they're buying into your vision. Don't let the tables get turned and end up with something other than what you have in your head and sold to your client unless everyone involved sees it as an improvement, and signs off on the changes, particularly your client.

The busier a director is, the less time they'll typically make for you, especially if they're an A-lister. That may not be the best scenario for getting what you need. If you find yourself doing a rushed preliminary call with a director from another set, and you don't have his or her full concentration, expect the same level of attention to your spot on the day of the shoot.

Some production companies keep their directors hustling at hyperdrive because everyone makes more cash that way. But that won't make your commercial any better. It puts you and your idea low on their list of priorities. There's a huge difference between a fast and decisive director and one who's shortcutting the process. Beware of directors who are constantly in a hurry. You need their complete focus, and you have every right to expect it.

Directors with big names who are too busy to go to initial auditions to direct the actors also present a giant red flag. You're paying the director for their time before and during production, not just for their involvement on the day of the big event.

DON'T BE SWAYED BY ARTISANAL ENCHILADAS AND HIPSTER TEES.

If people are handing you T-shirts and free merch they could be throwing up a smokescreen. A discharge-printed T-shirt shouldn't be the only well-produced piece you get out of the deal. Keep your eye on the ball.

You want to make smart choices in all aspects of the production, such as editors and sound composers. The same advice applies to animated spots.

Let's not forget about your voiceover talent. A great voice actor can make a big difference. But before you fall in love with the idea of a celebrity voiceover, remember they don't come cheap. Plus, their time is usually quite limited. They may be in "mail-it-in" mode when you need them in "nail-the-read" mode. Not every actor sees VO work as anything more than a cash grab.

What's more, their hefty price tag can take a huge bite out of your production budget. That money may be better spent on a voice that takes their job seriously, is available based on your schedule, and shows up without an I've-got-important-places-to-be attitude.

That said, I've found that most big-name actors I've cast have been reasonable to work with, although in many cases their time tends to be micromanaged by personal assistants, or agents who don't have the best interests of your commercial at heart.

The only agenda that should matter to you or your vendors is your idea. Everything else is smoke, mirrors, and window dressing. Getting your concepts produced as well as humanly possible is the only thing you should be focused on. That's your job.

Choose your vendors wisely, and you'll have the tools you need to succeed.

Yep. It's Storytime.

[NOTE: The director's name in the following story has been changed. After all, nobody wants to be dragged into court by a donkey.]

Just say "no" to Toby O'Toole

Allow me to set this story in its proper context. The year was 2004. Chrysler, in an attempt to take their brand upmarket, had outsourced the TV launch of their Pacifica to Arnell Group, a New York agency that was gaining a reputation for work on upscale brands. The resulting commercials, starring Celine Dion, were beautiful to look at – but a complete dud that infuriated dealers, as in their minds it targeted the wrong demographic and failed to convey the Mercedes-derived technology that Chrysler's new vehicles now had.

In accepting the lead position at BBDO in charge of all Chrysler brand creative, I was charged with correcting Arnell's strategic oversight, and wresting the creative back to BBDO. It was a messy situation. Peter Arnell, a charismatic handful, had blown his big shot and the bloom was off his rose. Everyone but Arnell himself could smell the writing on the walls.

We needed to immediately move away from Celine, whose only skin in the game was contractual. The Pacifica's overlooked features were pretty impressive at the time, as it was the first Chrysler to inherit shared technology from Mercedes. It was packed with next-level luxuries and state-of-the-art technology, including AWD, high-end audio, DVD monitors, a voice-activated navigation system, and Bluetooth.

The interior comfort was pretty damn amazing, too. My 6'5" frame fit comfortably into the Pacifica's second row with plenty of room to spare, and its third-row bench seat could easily hold additional passengers or cargo. None of those benefits were coming through in Arnell's arty black-and-white spots.

I conceived two spots that pushed the Pacifica far from celebrity soccer-mom territory.

In one spot, a Pacifica carrying six dudes was making its way down a snow-covered mountain road, the wind howling outside as the all-wheel-drive vehicle made easy work of the inclement weather and treacherous conditions. Meanwhile, the passengers inside were all riding in comfort, two of them watching a DVD screen, one sleeping, another writing in his journal with headphones on as the Pacifica deftly passed numerous vehicles stuck on the sides of the snowy mountain road.

The final reveal was the Pacifica reaching the base of the mountain and pulling into a commuter lot filled with perfectly adequate 4-wheel drive vehicles that had been granted the weekend off, thanks to the comfort and capability of the new Chrysler Pacifica.

A second Pacifica spot was conceived for warmer weather belts. It revolved around an athletic couple in the comfort of their new Pacifica, pulling up to a parking area at the base of a mountain biking trail. The spot nicely highlighted Pacifica's interior. Once parked at the foot of a biking trail, this spot's reveal featured an aggressive trail rider jumping over the vehicle captured through its moonroof, prompting the Pacifica's male passenger to suggest brunch at a nearby bistro before they embarked on their ride.

Fast forward to a happy client who felt that both ideas checked off a lot of necessary boxes, and properly conveyed the Pacifica as an upscale crossover vehicle. The two Pacifica spots were approved by Chrysler's director of marketing – the third person to inherit that role in less than a year. More on that, elsewhere.

We had a healthy budget by combining the two spots as a package. A commercial director rep I'd met in Detroit told me that he knew the perfect person to shoot our spots. He asked me to fasten my seat belt before he revealed the A-lister's name.

"I can get you Toby O'Toole!"

I knew the name. It was attached to some epic TV commercials. Unfortunately, the man had a horrible reputation. As fortune would have it, BBDO's Jeep group had recently used him without any issues, so I approached the idea with at least a semblance of comfort. "He used to be crazy," O'Toole's rep continued, "but he's calmed down a lot since his epic battle with the studio over the final cut of his first feature film. It would be a coup for you if you got him to shoot your spots."

I was starting to see his logic.

I had no inkling at the time that Toby O'Toole had bled his bank account dry running 35 full-page print ads in the Hollywood trade papers blasting the film studio who hired him for destroying the director's cut of "his" debut movie. Nor that O'Toole was lobbying the Directors Guild of America to remove his name from the end credits of his first feature film and replace it with "Humpty Dumpty." In retrospect, the battle over artistic control with the studio had all but destroyed his potential as a feature-film director.

Suffice to say that commercial reps can't be counted on to share all the details when they're trying to sell you a tool. I made a foolish decision without doing enough homework beyond a cursory endorsement from BBDO's Jeep team.

During a cordial conversation with O'Toole and his people about the two spots we had sold through. I made sure to point out that the spots were product-driven stories. Unlike the Celine Dion launch spots, our commercials needed to show plenty of functionality.

O'Toole made all the right noises and both myself and our executive producer took a deep breath and awarded the package to him.

Fast forward to the shoot. Everything was going well. The more difficult winter spot was in the can. That just left the less demanding spot to shoot. I felt confident we were going to deliver the goods. As O'Toole rehearsed the scene with the mountain bike flyover, I took a moment to walk up to the top of a mountain to get cell reception on my phone. I placed a call home. As I was checking in with my wife, I suddenly heard a man's voice screaming. I hung up immediately when I realized O'Toole was having a meltdown. His choice of words was horrific.

"You FUCKING C@*T!!! You FUCKING C@*T!!!"

Reaching the bottom of the hill, I found the entire crew staring at the ground as Toby O'Toole eviscerated his line producer in front of everyone. She was sobbing uncontrollably. BBDO's producer was as white as the snow we'd shot the day before when O'Toole had been on his best behavior. Today, he unraveled all that goodwill by going ballistic over a mountain-bike rider who had missed his mark in rehearsal.

Despite O'Toole's meltdown, we finished out the day with everyone walking on eggshells and it appeared we'd gotten the footage we needed. I allowed myself cautious optimism, which proved short-lived. I soon discovered that O'Toole was on his own personal crusade to create director's cuts that had nothing to do with our approved concepts. The man was clearly out to lunch.

As we were trying to get the cuts we sold our client cobbled together, Toby was lobbying for his own warped vision. He was burning the client's edit time working on cuts the client hadn't seen or approved. O'Toole had no interest in contributing to the process of delivering what we had sold our client.

Ironically, my salvation came in the form of a different tool, my newly appointed director of marketing who'd screwed the pooch even worse than I had. In his mad dash to get the new Pacifica spots on the air, he glossed over getting final approval from the German higher-ups at Daimler Benz. What he deemed a mere formality led to two commercials being killed in post-production.

It was the luckiest card I've ever been dealt. The entire production was shelved, and I walked away from a living nightmare unscathed. The rough cuts were never even asked for.

We returned to Detroit without finishing either spot. Back at BBDO, I beelined to the CCO and told him I had an epiphany during post-production. It was time for me to go back to Austin, to my family and friends. Back to the relative sanity of being a freelancer rather than a general in a battle against the Germans that no one could possibly win.

I'd survived three directors of marketing in less than a year, and the worst commercial director ordeal of my career. I was done working with directors of marketing who exploded with greater frequency than Spinal Tap drummers.

Game over.

My advice here is twofold. One, using the right tools for the job is vital to your success. So, pay attention to reputations; don't overlook a bad one in pursuit of production glory. And two, stay the fuck away from Toby O'Toole.

TIPS FOR CHOOSING THE RIGHT PRODUCTION PARTNERS.

- If an A-list director "loves your spot," make sure it's your spot they've fallen in love with. The bigger their name, the less likely they are to care what your vision is. Make sure their vision for your spot coincides with your own.

- What a younger director lacks in experience can be made up for in passion and accessibility. Be loyal if you find one you work well with, even as your budgets increase. Mutual trust is a valuable asset.

- Beware of directors, agency producers, and creative directors with agendas that don't benefit your idea. Always watch your idea's back.

- Soak up every ounce of wisdom you can from your agency producers and vendors. They can be great mentors and know more about film, audio, and editing than anyone else in the building.

- A-list directors can come with their own baggage. And therein lies the rub. They should be carrying your baggage, not vice versa.

- Bad reputations don't create themselves. Never sacrifice your own career trying to resurrect someone else's. If you take a risk on damaged goods, you will ultimately have only yourself to blame when it blows up in your face.

- The wisdom of a seasoned crew combined with the passion of a new director can be a killer combination if you're working with a challenging budget.

- Young editors save you money but take more time. Seasoned vets are faster and, in some cases, are worth the additional cost.

- Don't let a creative director take over your idea, and leave you in the weeds. Stay attached to your idea at all costs. That's where you learn the things that no ad class will teach you.

- Celebrities can be class acts or spoiled brats. Don't ever let a celebrity shortchange your project because they have better places to be.

NEVER FALL IN LOVE WITH THE SMELL OF **MEDIOCRITY**

In a perfect ad world, the biggest and best ideas would always win. That happens more times than not at the best agencies. That's how they become the best agencies. They refuse to present straw dogs. They back the strongest ideas through the entire production, leveraging the best people for the job every step of the way. Everyone who touches the idea contributes to making it better.

And then we have the other type of agency, where the best ideas never win. Where you just can't win. Where the only thing you get from swinging for the fences is a damaged rotator cuff.

Many big accounts try to appease everyone without pissing anyone off. That's an agenda that poses a real problem to advertising creatives trying to advance their careers on the strength of great produced work.

There's a reason why mediocre agencies exist.

THERE'S A HUGE DEMAND FOR MEDIOCRE.

The sad truth is, a lot of clients strive to produce work that never gets talked about. After all, mediocre work rarely causes controversy or gets a client fired. It's a messed-up world where clients and agencies are rewarded for being spineless while the most creative shops are constantly on the hot seat for doing courageous, outrageous stuff that gets talked about and debated. Playing to not lose is the unfortunate philosophy of all too many agencies.

Don't hitch your wagon to an agency or a boss who is timid and afraid to rock the boat. You'll never rock your portfolio.

A CREATIVE DIRECTOR CAN ONLY BE AS GOOD AS THE AGENCY THAT HIRES THEM.

Beware of big, dumb agencies with big,dumb accounts. Sure, they say they want better thinking but just try giving it to them. If an agency spends all its energy working within a client's comfort zone and is afraid to show out-of-the-box thinking, they're likely more concerned with protecting billings and their precious bottom line than building or maintaining a strong creative reputation.

It doesn't make them terrible people. But, it can make the agency a tough place for you to make a name for yourself. The world is full of clients who care more about surviving to their next paychecks than doing great work. No creative director can sell great work to a client who is in constant cover-thy-ass mode. Neither can you.

Find an agency that prides itself on doing great work, and you'll be far more likely to do the kind of work that will propel your career.

LEVEL PLAYING FIELDS EXIST. FIND ONE.

As a creative director, I always backed the best idea, no matter where it came from. Not the idea the client will be most likely to buy, or the idea that makes the account team the most comfortable. The best idea.

The great Bill Bernbach, a hero to my dad's generation and the force behind many breakthrough campaigns that defined the 60's advertising era said it best. "Don't tell me the right thing. Tell me the inspiring thing." Ideas that try to do it all are rarely worth a rip. Look for the nugget that's most likely to be remembered. The idea that's true to the client's cultural DNA, and builds their brand. I've found no better way to build my own brand.

Unfortunately, that's not how all creative directors roll. Some play favorites and throw bones to the bootlickers. Some play petty politics. Some force their sensibilities upon their clients. Others employ the cowardly move and defer to the account people to make the call.

Creativity is purely subjective. But, if you feel that your best thinking is constantly being overlooked, you owe it to yourself to find a creative director who plays fair at an agency that not only believes in great work but can sell and produce it.

Level playing fields do exist. I encourage you to find one.

DR. FRANKENSTEIN DIDN'T LET A LITTLE THING LIKE DEATH KEEP HIS IDEAS FROM LIVING.

The mark of a real pro is someone who does something good with every opportunity, regardless of the situation. Whether the agency or client is perceived as good or bad. Whether the client is neurotic or made of Teflon. If you can always manage to do something good even when the odds are stacked against you, you will have a great career.

Just don't expect anyone else to steer you into the promised land of creative excellence, rainbows, and unicorns. It's your job to keep your portfolio progressing. If you're not doing the kind of work that advances your portfolio, it's up to you to figure out why and course-correct as soon as possible. With that in mind, let's identify a few potential barriers, and discuss what you can do to overcome them.

DOES YOUR CREATIVE DIRECTOR HAVE NO BUSINESS JUDGING CREATIVE? UH-OH.

It's a bitter pill to swallow, but your boss may not know good from bad. It happens all the time. Incompetant people get promoted, as they tend to be easier for other incompetent people to play with. Complacency is commonplace, particularly with massive accounts that cover a lot of salaries.

Mediocrity has a way of breeding like bunnies in the ad business. Don't get pulled toward it, no matter how fluffy your boss is, or how many carrots he or she dangles in front of you. Carrots don't build your portfolio. I've made the mistake of working for bosses who possessed stunning people skills and major presentation chops, but who couldn't creative direct their way out of a wet paper bag. Even if I liked them as people, they didn't do me any favors from a career standpoint.

The wrong boss can teach you bad habits that are hard to break, like second-guessing the work, compromising the creative for the sake of smoother client meetings, or bad-mouthing clients or the account people in front of the troops.

If your creative director is weak, overly political, or afraid of work that pushes beyond the ordinary, you'll never produce anything great working for him or her. Find a better boss. Even if that boss is an asshole.

GIVE ME A FLAMING ASSHOLE OVER A SPINELESS BOOTLICKER ANY DAY OF THE WEEK.

Another possible barrier to your success can be superiors who can recognize great work but don't have the stones to back it. This is a bad sign on all fronts. They have no qualms about advancing their careers through less courageous thinking.

Chances are, they're compromising and capitulating to their clients because they think that's the winning formula for keeping their jobs.

I've had bosses who were creative as hell when working under other creative directors, but were weak once they were handed the reins. The most competent creative can be a total dud as a leader. The ability to be highly creative and sell the best work doesn't always go hand in hand. Creatives often rise to the level of their incompetence. Once there, they begin politicking, bluffing, or hedging all bets to stay on top. Their insecurities and fears prevent them from backing the kind of thinking that built their portfolios.

Don't tether yourself to a boss who has traded in their courage card for a big mortgage, a fancy car, or a spouse who spends money like a kid in a candy store. Call a headhunter. Seek higher ground. You can't fix a boss who has creatively cashed in their chips.

AVOID GETTING TRAPPED BENEATH AN EGOMANIAC ON THE ORG CHART.

What keeps a creative director from letting the best ideas rise to the top? Sometimes it's their own fragile ego. Perhaps they got stood up at the prom, and never got over it. Who the hell knows? It's their problem, not yours.

If you work for an asshole, make sure you're getting great work to show for it. Sometimes, it's worth every ounce of anguish if it advances your career. It can also help you develop a thicker skin, which means you'll be able to endure more torture than other creatives. If you can master the art of working for an asshole without becoming one yourself, you can pretty much work for anyone without getting your feathers ruffled.

But never stay in a job in hopes that your asshole boss will wake up one day and magically respect others. Don't kid yourself they're going to mellow with age. Learn everything you can, but know this. If working for an asshole is causing you sleepless nights, you need to find a shop with a more creatively secure individual at the helm.

LOAD GUN. AIM CAREFULLY. SHOOT FOOT.

Which leads me to perhaps the most painful possibility of all. It could be that you're the one killing your dream. Yeah, you.

You might be making the mistake of thinking that your shit doesn't stink. Maybe you're too blinded by ambition and pride to admit you're constantly being bested by better thinking. The warning signs may include no one appreciating your thinking, people trying to modify your ideas all the time, or you being the only one in your department who isn't consistently delivering.

It's one thing to fall in love with some of your ideas. But it's another thing to think all of your work is the best stuff on the table every time. That gets old fast and for everyone in the room. My advice? Gather up half a dozen of your best ideas that got killed, find someone whose talent is beyond reproach, and ask them to take a look and level with you. Tough medicine, for sure. But it might be necessary if you're going to pull yourself from the wreckage of your own arrogance.

DON'T IGNORE THE WRITING ON THE WALL, ESPECIALLY IF IT'S ABOUT YOU.

If you recognize any of the scenarios I've just spelled out, do your career a favor. Change your situation, your mindset, or both as soon as humanly possible.

What really matters here is your future and moving forward in the most productive way possible. Find an agency where the best ideas win, even if they're not always yours. Trust the people who hired you to tell you the truth. Learn everything you can from those around you. Push yourself harder no matter how much it hurts. Develop a reputation for never giving up. Don't hesitate to give others credit when they beat you with better thinking. And if someone else provides you with the spark that leads to your big breakthrough, by all means, give them credit. That's how the best creatives roll.

Find and help foster that kind of environment and you'll not only be at a better place, but you'll also be the kind of person who deserves it.

And, with that, it's Storytime.

The Super Bowl spot that wouldn't leave the bowl

The agency I was at was deep in the throes of the dotcom boom and the creative department was busier than a one-legged man in an ass-kicking contest. All of corporate America had discovered the Internet. Capitalists were circling online business models like sharks. Clients were snapping up URLs like hotcakes, and everyone was looking to turn the web into untold riches.

The IPO cash grab was at its zenith.

We had half a dozen dotcoms walk in the door in one year alone. Ask.com. Dr.Koop.com. Hoovers.com. Gotomeeting.com. There were more but my head hurts just thinking about them. For the most part, these companies didn't give two shits about conflicts of interest or bona fide branding. All they cared about was generating buzz, and hitting the IPO jackpot.

Our agency was cranking out dotcom work like a widget factory. I'm pretty sure the principals were trading free creative for a piece of the action because no one seemed to care how hard the creative department was hustling. It was all about the Benjamins, except for us poor schlubs creating the work. I was on the grinding end of that spectrum along with every creative in the building.

One day, word spread that one of our newest dotcom clients – known as gotomeeting.com – had popped for a Super Bowl spot. The national media buy was made, and the agency was licking their chops for a chance to make it to the big show. Their first nationally televised spot would soon be on the biggest game of all, The Super Bowl.

Although the client's service offered businesses something of real value, it was hardly sexy stuff. An online meeting facilitator, Go-to-meeting's website functioned as an organizational hub allowing people to coordinate and collaborate from remote locations.

The agency, over 500 people strong at the time, was split into four independent creative groups. The GCD team overseeing the assignment wasn't hitting pay dirt, so it was opened up to all GCDs in the agency for a high-stakes creative shootout.

Even though everyone was tired, the words "Super" and "Bowl" managed to summon everyone's attention. It certainly caught mine. I had only one problem. My GCD partner couldn't work that weekend, and the internal check-in was on Monday. So, I went to GSD&M's creative services manager and presented my case. "I want you to hire a freelancer to work with me over the weekend. Let me book the best creative I know." I then informed the creative services manager that Kathy Hepinstall was available.

"Wait a minute, isn't she a writer? Why would we team up two writers?"

More hemming and hawing ensued. I stuck to my guns. "I've known Kathy for years, I trust her talent, and her work speaks for itself. We need a Big Idea, or the agency is going to look like bozos. The creative services manager finally relented. "Fine," he said, "but you'd better come through."

I sent Kathy the brief, and we went through it. Gotomeeting.com championed small to medium "enterprise" businesses by allowing employees to collaborate remotely, precisely what Kathy and I were now doing. We agreed to each spend some time thinking about it and to hop on the phone the next day. It was Saturday afternoon when Kathy called. I had jotted down my initial thinking and was ready to share.

Kathy went first.

"I think I have something really cool... what if our Super Bowl spot was a bunch of small businesses collaborating to make sure the Super Bowl goes off without a hitch?" Kathy's big, beautiful brain had thrown the perfect Hail Mary. All I had to do was let it drop into my hands, and run with it. We quickly went over other ideas, my own included, but her initial idea was the gem. Kathy sent me a treatment. I tweaked it a little, sent it back, and then Kathy wrote the script.

Cut to Monday's internal creative review, led by a seasoned GCD team.

Several teams presented thinking. When it was my turn, I zeroed in on what made our approach unique. Whereas most of the other teams followed the brief to the letter by leveraging empowerment, Kathy and I would demonstrate how GoToMeeting.com's innovative technology worked in reality.

"Our idea is a product demo, pure and simple," I began, "...we're going to show GoToMeeting in use, then reveal a surprise ending." Our script opened with people working remotely, using our client's site to coordinate their efforts. We don't know what project they're working on. We cut from one person to another. "I'll requisition 10,340 rolls of two-ply toilet paper." "I'll order 25,000 pure beef franks." "I'll secure 25,000 foam fingers." "At the end of the spot," I concluded, "the project all these people are working together on turns out to be the Super Bowl itself".

You could have heard a pin drop.

Everyone in the room that day knew it was a great idea. It was unlike any Super Bowl spot, ever. A Super Bowl spot about the making of the Super Bowl. The GCDs running the pitch pulled me aside and thanked me profusely. I, of course, had Kathy to thank for it. By hiring the right person, I was able to support great thinking without dropping the ball. All I had to do was punch it into the end zone from the two-yard line.

Our idea went to the client meeting along with two others. The GCD team, who'd been toiling on the assignment for a month of Sundays, also had a direction in the mix. The client liked two of the three ideas, ours being one of them. Asked which the GCDs preferred, they recommended theirs.

I was pissed.

Not pissed that we'd been beaten. Being beaten is part of the game. I was pissed by what we'd been beaten by. An idea that I wouldn't have recommended, or even shown to a client if it had been my call. The GCDs sold the client on having a montage of "empowered" small business owners singing the Queen song "We Are the Champions." Fuuuuuuuccckkkk.

Yes, it was dead-on brief. More so than our idea, to be frank. But, it leaned heavily on having a bunch of actors posing as businesspeople butchering a beloved rock anthem that already gets overplayed in every sports arena on the planet. A karaoke of a tired sports cliché on the day of the big game.

I'll say it again. Fuuuuuuuccckkkk!!!!

Fast forward. The song was negotiated for and publishing rights were paid. Bank accounts got padded. The commercial was shot, and it dropped like a bomb on the big day. Post-Super Bowl ad polls placed "We Are the Champions" in the basement of their "bad" lists. Nobody got a ticker-tape parade, least of all the GCD team who came up with it.

The agency suffered further humiliation when Adweek's Annual Agency Report Card came out at year's end, and the agency's creative grade was lowered from the prior year based on our insipid Super Bowl spot. It was suggested that the agency was losing its spark.

There wasn't a hole in the ground big enough for the agency to fit into.

The moral here is simple. On any given day, anyone's thinking can stink up the joint, your own included. The trick is to know it, and back the best work, whether it's yours or someone else's.

Now let's do our best to flush this subject and move on.

TIPS ON PITFALLS TO ACTIVELY AVOID

- Your career depends on the judgment of others. Make sure your bosses have decent judgment.

- Be wary of agencies where the best ideas never win. That could be part of their business model.

- Don't let your ego cloud your judgment. Find an agency that champions the best ideas regardless of where they come from.

- Babysit the shit out of Super Bowl assignments. Too many eyeballs, petty agendas, and nervous hand-wringing can spoil even the best idea.

- Always have a contingency plan for generating big ideas. Keep the Ernie Schencks and Kathy Hepinstalls of the world on speed dial.

- If you produce a killer Super Bowl spot, you might be remembered for it. If you drop the ball on a Super Bowl spot, you will most definitely be remembered.

- Everyone's shit stinks sometimes. Even yours.

KNOW THE TRUE VALUE OF WHAT YOU'RE SELLING. **STARTING WITH YOURSELF**

Getting paid what you're worth is important. Whether it's a salary at a starting gig, or your rate as a freelancer, establishing your value is crucial. Ask too little, and you can come off as lacking confidence. Ask too much, and people will think you believe that you're the next David Droga.

Give some serious thought to your worth before you're asked to place a price on your head.

As I see it, it's an answer that should be based on how long you've been in the business, how prolific you are, and how persuasive you can be when discussing your abilities.

THE REAL VALUE OF ANY ITEM IS WHAT SOMEONE IS WILLING TO PAY FOR IT.

If you don't know the going rate at your level or for a particular market, a good headhunter is a valuable person to know. They can offer you the benefit of their perspective, particularly if they like you and your work. By seeking their advice, you can build a respectful and solid relationship. One you can both benefit from in the future.

Headhunters also know who's hiring, where the best work is being done, and who the best bosses are. They can point you in the right direction, and offer valuable guidance that your professors and parents can't. They are closer to the pulse. Unless, of course, you have an insider's perspective like I did. But enough about that for now. This is about you and making sure you get paid what you're worth.

To that end, always pay attention to the cost of living where you accept your first job, as it can vary wildly. Remember that your salary will be relative to the cost of living. A solid offer in one market can be a terrible one in a more expensive city. Make sure you do your homework.

Again, this is where a good headhunter can be of value.

IF YOU'RE LUCKY, YOU'LL START YOUR CAREER MAKING LESS THAN YOUR FRIENDS.

Great shops often pay less than mediocre ones. And rightfully so. They understand you'll make more money at your next job simply by having their name on your resume, and the kind of work they're known for in your portfolio. This is particularly true if you're fortunate enough to get great work produced. A single high-profile campaign – a Cannes Lion winner, for instance – can increase your visibility and market value and put you on the radar of the best agencies in the world.

STEP RIGHT UP AND COLLECT YOUR FREE PUNCH IN THE FACE.

Beware of bottom feeders who work for great agencies. In-house talent coordinators who offer you next to nothing, or expect you to take a huge pay cut, for the privilege of working at their agency. For reasons I've never been able to fathom, people like that are somehow able to continue to attract unsuspecting victims who just want to create cool work.

These opportunists typically leverage their clients, the award-winning work the agency has done, and the chance for you to bolster your reputation.

What's worse is the fact that, since they're often walking profit centers for their agencies, their gambit is quietly tolerated. Often, they'll try to use their agency's perception as a bargaining chip. "If you work for us, it's great exposure for you." Yeah, right.

The sad truth is, they rarely will reward you with more opportunities if you agree to their crappy terms. They're too busy scrounging for the next sucker. What they're doing is taking unfair advantage of talented people who lack the experience to know they're being duped.

NOTHING PLUS NOTHING IS NOTHING.

If anyone asks you to work for dirt cheap, ask them how far below market value they're paid. Whether they acknowledge your point or not, it sends a signal: you understand that you bring value, and you're not up for being hosed. In the immortal words of my dad, "Never give your thinking away for free. It devalues you, and you end up being worth exactly what you're being paid. Nothing"

If someone can't see the value of your thinking by looking at your portfolio, they'll never see it. **Master the art of saying "thanks, but no thanks" early in your career.** Don't get talked into a sucky deal unless the end completely justifies the means. If you're going to work for below your value, make damn sure that you have a good run to show for it.

That said, it's Storytime.

Only an idiot works for free. I speak from experience

Years ago, I was asked by a freelance art director to take a gamble and work on a spec pitch for a friend of his. It was someone he knew and trusted. We needed to win a pitch, then produce the work before anyone would see a payday. But it promised a tidy payout at the end of the rainbow, and the assignment appeared infinitely winnable based on a solid brief.

Since I had bandwidth at the time, I agreed to the quick turnaround. That's the problem with appearances. They're deceiving little bastards. I had no idea what I was getting myself into. The assignment was for Microsoft, who was launching its new Lumia 635 smartphone with a state-of-the-art voice recognition system. It did a host of things Siri should have done well but didn't.

Apple had just launched a high-profile TV campaign for Siri featuring Samuel L. Jackson, John Malkovich, Zooey Deschanel, and other random celebrities, each using Siri to get weather reports, directions, even the ingredients for risotto.

But the truth of the matter was Apple had uncharacteristically jumped the gun. Siri users, no matter how devout, found Siri to be buggier than bird droppings. It was a rare misstep for Apple, and Microsoft had a narrow window to plant their flag and lay claim to a superior voice command system before Apple shored up Siri's nagging issues.

An assignment was lobbed out to Northern California social and digital shops, and three agencies found themselves in the final running for the assignment. One of those agencies was a dark horse, a "virtual agency" devised by a San Francisco-based planner who'd leveraged a client relationship to get in on the pitch.

In other words, us.

As fortune would have it, our pitch idea won the assignment. It looked like a nice payday was in my very near future. The winning idea centered on a short web film featuring disenchanted Siri users sharing their relationship problems in a confessional manner.

After "winning" the assignment, one of the clients pointed out that our idea was close to something that had already been done in the smartphone category. Much to our disappointment, the client was right.

In an effort to help, the client suggested we treat the idea as a group therapy session instead of separate vignettes of people carping about their relationships. My partners balked at the suggestion.

I felt the suggestion had merit, and it absolutely solved the problem of the idea seeming derivative. It made the idea more interesting, albeit much harder to pull off. After I cobbled together the new treatment, we realized the client's suggestion solved one problem while creating an entirely new one. It was far more ambitious in scope.

We took a deep collective breath and shared the new idea with our client. Not surprisingly, they dug it. After all, it was based on their suggestion. On our recommendation, the client agreed to take the revised concept to upper management and lobby for an additional $50k to cover the more ambitious production. In addition to more actors, the back-and-forth dialogue and reaction shots would require a more comprehensive production and edit.

That's when fate intervened. One faction at Microsoft felt that poking fun at Apple was a dangerous tactic, and wanted to kill the initiative altogether, especially since it was going to cost more. None of us had made a dime, and we were now perilously close to watching the assignment evaporate before our very eyes.

Welcome to the dangers of working for free.

We barely managed to keep the idea on life support by begrudgingly agreeing to make the existing budget work. In a jam over who we could get to produce the film, I thought of my colleague, Sam Miller, who'd shot a handful of regional spots for me in Denver. Sam was a good young Director of Photography/Director who'd come up through the editing ranks, and he shared my appreciation for subtlety when it comes to humor.

I gave Sam a call and sent him the script. He told us exactly what we'd hoped to hear. "I could definitely use a Microsoft piece on my reel, even if it's break-even for me. I can direct and edit it. Let me try to make the numbers work."

Instead of what should have been a two-day shoot, Sam devised a plan to shoot the whole thing in one long day in Los Angeles by having two cameras with a second DP shooting coverage, so we could capture on-camera dialogue and reactions from others in the room simultaneously.

We slashed our travel budget to the bone, removing hotels and good meals from the equation. We shot one day in L.A. and finished in San Francisco using an edit facility that Sam Miller could access at a reduced rate. We cut corners everywhere and put as much budget as we could into the film. Despite the challenges, Sam shot and cut the film together beautifully. "Siri Group Therapy" hit the web with pre-roll teasers, and rapidly racked up two million views, performing three times better than any viral piece in Microsoft's history.

In my four days staying in the Tenderloin district of SF while finishing the film, I chipped my tooth on a slice of pizza, survived the biggest earthquake since the San Francisco-Oakland Bay Bridge dropped in '89, and stepped in human feces while walking to the edit facility one morning. I also had my laptop stolen from our car while it was parked in broad daylight.

All of that considered, I still didn't regret it. The film came out nice and was a great piece for all involved. Sam Miller got a great short film, Microsoft wrote the check, and nobody missed any meals.

But to be honest, if I took a hard look at the amount of personal time and effort I expended to get this production done right, I didn't make what I'm worth. And even worse, I had to pull a ton of favors from personal contacts to get the job done.

It sucks getting paid less than you're worth. It sucks more when you have to call in favors from your friends and colleagues to get work produced for companies who have deep pockets.

But what monumentally sucks is when you take an active role in doing it to yourself. So don't.

TIPS FOR KEEPING YOUR WITS ABOUT YOU, AND YOUR WORK

- Never work for free. The client and agency are getting paid well. Why should you be cut out?

- Be creative about where you stay and eat, and the money you spend when on production. Sometimes you're better off putting the money where you can see it.

- Be an extra set of hands in production if help is needed, and stay out of the way if it isn't.

- Work with people you trust. Find people who share your sensibilities, and stick with them. They have your back, and you have theirs. Leverage those relationships every chance you get.

- Never assume that a client is willing to spend more because they're one of the wealthiest corporations in the world. They're a business, too.

- Always listen carefully to a client's suggestions. Sometimes they really can make a good idea better.

- If you ask a director to invest in your idea when you've got a challenging budget, be willing to reciprocate when you have a good board and a better budget. Loyalty is a two-way street.

DON'T JUDGE
A BOOK BY ITS
FOOSBALL TABLE

Sometimes, you find yourself at a restaurant where they have loud funky music, servers in trendy garb, and all sorts of oddities hanging on the walls. Pretty dazzling, isn't it? Until the moment the food arrives. It's right then, when you've got a mouthful of microwaved chicken fajita, that you realize all the hoopla is meant to distract you from the barely edible truth.

It's all a smokescreen.

Many agencies are a lot like that, too. Their front door is shaped like a giant light bulb, their lobby is filled with chairs that look like silver marshmallows, and the receptionist is wearing more makeup than a mime.

Then you get a look at the work. It's not painful, but it's uninspired and looks like it came off an assembly line. The client list is full of big, safe, corporate accounts that no one gives a shit about creatively, but the clients pay their bills on time and just look at those hipster chairs. The lobby alone proves my point. It has to be a stunning piece of work because there's no stunning work to show.

GREAT WORK. IT'S THE ULTIMATE SHINY OBJECT.

Across town is an agency that could not be more different from the one with the carnival midway masquerading as a lobby. Their digs are functional at best, their parking lot is small, and their desks are 1998-era IKEA. But on the wall, you see what they're actually about. Eye-catching, smart, funny, daring, and well-crafted work. Ideas. Loads of them.

Ideas someone took the time to beautifully
execute rather than simply push out like
extruded sausage. It's all killer and no filler.
No smoke and mirrors are needed in this lobby
to tell you what this agency stands for.

We stand by our work. Ideas are our art.
Our clients are our benefactors.

Great work is the most impressive decor an
agency can have. Look for it, and don't fall for
the thin veneer of a compromise factory
posing as a creative workspace.

DON'T GET TALKED INTO A FULL-TIME JOB
WORKING FOR A TEMPORARY FIXTURE.

Another trap to beware of is taking a job to
work for a specific individual. Granted, he or
she may be an amazing salesperson, charming
as hell, and promise you an opportunity that
you just can't ignore. Unless their name is on
the door, they are not a permanent fixture.
Anyone can be fired, lured away, or replaced
without notice.

People move. So, do some simple subtraction
in your head before you make a rash decision.
Look at the agency holistically, and imagine
what the job would be like without your boss. If
it ceases to look like a golden opportunity, take
that into consideration. Maybe it's more of a
silver or bronze opportunity. It still may
be worth a shot.

But, if it all looks a bit grey and uninspiring
without the one person trying to win you over,
trust your gut. If it's only as good as the person
who hires you, you might want to think twice
before signing on. At least be prepared for
what you're walking into.

Another thing to beware of is an agency
whose work lacks consistency. If the only
good work is being done for just one particular
account, consider how many people will be
clamoring for those same assignments. You
may be saving yourself a world of occupational
suffering by thinking twice about an agency
with spotty work. Always look at the worst
work coming out of the agency. Don't be fooled
by superficial lobby porn.

Shiny knives can have extremely dull blades.

That said, it's Storytime.

Guess where they're planning to blow that smoke?

In 2010, I was contacted by a headhunter about an ECD gig at an agency in Denver. I'd never heard of the place before. I soon learned that it was a new agency network stitched together from a handful of smaller agencies with a charismatic global chief creative officer at the forefront who had an ambitious growth plan.

Making no promises, I flew to Denver for an interview.

Other than an epic view overlooking downtown Denver and the Rocky Mountains, the office was uninspiring, drab, and boring. I tried to be polite about it, but in my humble opinion, the agency's creative fit the same description as their generic digs.

I spent the better part of the day meeting with the office's principals: a president who I instantly liked, a seasoned strategic planner who struck me as intelligent and capable, and his wife, the highest-ranking account person in the agency.

Bea Fromell, we'll call her, for reasons soon to be revealed.

Bea spent the lion's share of our time together telling me about the Denver office's largest account, and its remarkable CEO, who had built an impressive culture.

The problem was, the work the agency had done for that client in no way leaned into all the remarkable things the client was doing right.

It was an easy opportunity to turn down and I politely did so. That's when the global CCO came after me with the intensity of a seasoned stalker. He was charismatic as hell and warmer than melted butter. He shared his master plan for the new network and significantly sweetened the offer.

Somewhere between the sweeter offer and the 20,000-foot smoke screen the CCO orchestrated for my benefit, I bought in. It's amazing how money, company stock and a global vision can impair your own.

The master plan included plush new digs as soon as the current lease expired. Somebody was going to get a perfectly nice dental office.

Denver had one of the largest single pieces of business in the entire network, and, as far as cultures go, the client was doing many things right in a category consumers despised: cable and internet providers. I knew I could course-correct their work, and with the global CCO's blessing, I set about making the work demonstrably better.

I soon discovered that the biggest hurdle facing our client wasn't the client. It was Bea. Just days after I'd joined, the Denver office's president, the one I liked so much, was unceremoniously pushed from the skyscraper by his unscrupulous partners, who he'd known and worked with for years. The remaining partners were playing a different game; creating marginal work, logging banker's hours, and cooking the numbers to justify their salaries. The pair had a completely different agenda than the global chief creative officer.

Worse yet, they shared a mortgage and a last name.

In retrospect, had I checked Glassdoor.com, I would've never stepped into the mess. Hindsight is every bit the bitch that Bea turned out to be. Always look at Glassdoor if you're interviewing at an agency. Always. Even if they're committed to change, you'll at least get a sense of what the place's problems are.

After torpedoing the agency's president, Bea laid claim to the president role. Her self-promotion told me everything I needed to know about the agency and my future there. I immediately pursued two paths. Rebranding the office's largest client, who I liked quite a bit, and finding a new gig.

Bea's first act as president involved slashing my creative department's hiring budget, deeming a senior ACD/writer position unnecessary. I was left with barely enough coin to hire one junior writer.

Bea was setting traps within days of her self-promotion and quickly proved to have no affinity for creative thinking. The more interesting an idea, the more personally threatened she was by it. Bea was a truly blunt object. "You're not showing that to my client", was a common reaction from her even when her husband, the henpecked head of planning, loved our thinking.

Welcome to my nightmare, to say nothing of his.

I nonetheless forged a strong working relationship with our largest client's CEO, a remarkable woman named Colleen, who deemed a soup-to-nuts repositioning campaign I'd spearheaded the best thing she'd ever had presented to her. Whew.

The new campaign ushered the brand into respectable territory and was well-received both internally and by consumers. It differentiated the brand and made the company human. It was the right campaign at the right time and moved the needle nicely, mixing illustration and live-action and working cohesively across all platforms.

It was also featured in The Fifty, the Denver Ad Club's yearly award show, which while certainly not as prestigious as a clutch of Gold Pencils at The One Show, was validation we were moving the once indistinctive work in the right direction.

You'd think Bea would have been happy. But that's not how people like her are wired.

Bea cornered me in the office one day and warned me I was receiving numerous complaints from staffers. She claimed her account people were unhappy with my newest junior writer, who was repeatedly questioning the briefs. I informed her that I'd encouraged him to do so because the briefs weren't evolving as nicely as the work.

We both knew the real truth behind that exchange.

Bea was losing her client's ear. While she was trying to protect billings and take no chances, busily comparing every communication to the industry playbook, I was building trust and taking the client's culture into ownable territory. Creating work with my teams that differentiated the brand and celebrated its culture.

Bea claimed I was spending too much time on our largest piece of business and informed me she would be personally leading the account, replacing me in all high-level meetings. That was not at all how it played out. The CEO of our biggest account asked that I be included in all decisions and I continued to over-deliver and sit in every meeting at the CEO's request.

That's the tragic thing about people like Bea. They're often so busy planning their next gutless move that they never take the time to truly serve their clients or concern themselves with differentiating the client's brand. Bea looked at clients as a commodity. A number. A necessary item on the balance sheet.

I managed to find a new gig just blocks from our office. An independent local agency had just lost their ECD and as fortune would have it, they had a decent roster. The dough was not on par with what I was making, but I knew it was a legit opportunity to escape a corrosive environment and do some nice work for a solid account roster.

In negotiating my deal, I added a stipulation. I'd be bringing a young writer with me. Yep, the same one Bea Fromell had been knifing in the back.

Let's just say our largest client's CEO was none too happy to hear about my exodus.

Fast forward. Within months, my old agency had relocated into cool new digs in the hippest part of town. But karmic justice prevailed, when my ex-client put her account into review, and moved the business to TDA in nearby Boulder.

Without the office's largest client to help float their lease, the agency took immediate action. Bea Fromell fell from the tree and nobody attempted to break her fall. They were too busy enjoying the flurry of snapping sounds.

TIPS FOR AVOIDING TOXIC ENVIRONMENTS

- Avoid taking a job solely for the chance to work for a specific person, no matter how amazing they are. If they leave, your main motive for being there will be gone.

- Always look at the work carefully. Is it respectable? If it isn't as good as the agency's office space, know that you're in for an uphill slog, with no relief in sight.

- Be courteous and professional to anyone who takes time to interview you, even if you don't want the job. You never know where they'll be in a year or two.

- Be careful when being pitched a job opportunity by a charismatic chief creative officer. Particularly if you won't be working with or reporting to that person directly.

- If a mediocre agency hires you to help improve their creative work, take a good look at the entire staff. You'll likely have no control over re-staffing other departments, and they could be a big part of the problem.

- Turning a bad agency around sometimes requires cutting cancer out at the very top. Agencies are rarely willing to look that far up the food chain until they're in really deep shit. By then, it's often a case of too little, too late.

- The better creative agencies invest in talent, not trendy furnishings. Don't mistake smoke and mirrors for actual substance. You can't put a cool space in your portfolio.

- It's essential to do your homework if you're offered a job at a place you're unfamiliar with. Check sites like Glassdoor.com as part of your discovery process.

- People on power trips are not to be trusted. Ever.

"HOLD MY WATCH AND BEER THIS"

[Ten bite-sized stories that didn't find their way into this book elsewhere, the first one written by my brother, a fellow advertising copywriter and the editor of this book.]

It's Okay to Change Tribes

There's no shame in being cast in the wrong role in advertising. If you darkly suspect you don't belong on the mound, consider switching positions. It's not unheard of if you're well-liked, and seen as a good cultural fit.

If you feel like you've been miscast, talk to your boss. See if there is any chance you can be transitioned. But, do so carefully. You don't want to talk yourself out of a job. Or, you could hope someone else recognizes your situation and gets you fired.

When I was working in San Francisco, there was a junior account executive I quite liked. For this story, we'll call him Jake. He was a truly interesting guy, with wry observations and dry wit. Although his skills were still developing, the aforementioned qualities came through in his emails and interoffice communications.

Trouble was, Jake was a shitty account person. He had no feel for the position, no patience for decorum, and no passion for his duties whatsoever.

It was clear he needed to be doing something else. So, I took it upon myself to get him fired. I had no real staffing power or influence. My boss and his partners were smart guys who made their own decisions.

But, I felt this situation needed addressing. So, I went into my boss's office one fateful day and made my case, detailing all the issues I'd witnessed with Jake's performance.

In summation, I told him flat out, "I really think you should fire Jake." My boss nodded his head wearily to signal agreement, clearly troubled by the prospect because, just like everyone else, he liked Jake, too. ". . . then immediately rehire him as a junior writer," I added.

Just as I had done in listing the negatives regarding his account skills, I laid out all the things that had me convinced he would make a terrific writer. I then offered to help him out on his journey.

In no time, he was hired by the creative department and went on to become a serious talent. A few years later, when the agency was in the dumps and jobs were on the line, I went to that same boss, and suggested that he fire me and promote Jake to a senior writer.

For the second time, he agreed.

(Reading my brother Bill's story reminded me of how my friend, George Chalekian, became a copywriter. So I'll take back the reins and share George's story).

Any Jerk Can Win

George Chalekian was our creative coordinator when I worked at Ogilvy & Mather/ Los Angeles. When not picking up dry cleaning for our impeccably dressed executive creative director, Ivan Horvath, making coffee, or otherwise herding us cats, George could be found with his nose buried deep in advertising awards annuals, learning everything he could about the creative process.

It was abundantly clear George was a creative at heart. But having taken an admin gig, his options were somewhat limited.

One day, a casino account rejected yet another round of billboard concepts the agency had presented for their slot machines. The visual was mandated by the client, which is a bad way to start a billboard assignment.

So, the creatives were limited to a picture of a slot machine, which may explain why the agency was having trouble cranking out something great. To be fair, one of the art directors had laid out an outdoor board with the slot machine's arm extending off the right side of the board, which at least lent it a bit of visual drama.

On this particular day, our charismatic executive creative director had a moment of divine inspiration. He decided that it was George Chalekian's time to shine. "If you can sell our client a great outdoor board, George," he boldly announced, "I'll make you a junior copywriter."

George came in the next day with a mountain of ideas. The poor kid had probably stayed up all night coming up with them. Failure would not be an option. At one point during the day, Ivan walked by George's desk, saw a stack of thinking, and realized that George had jumped the conceptual shark. He summarily informed George that he didn't have the time to look at all of George's ideas.

"Just show me your best one, George."

Not missing a beat, George held up the first idea in his stack. The line he had written couldn't have been simpler, or fit the layout more perfectly.

"Any Jerk Can Win"

Ivan stared at it in stunned silence, then flashed his big, beautiful Hungarian smile. "Very good, George. Now let's go find you an office." I don't recall for the life of me if the client bought the board, but there was no denying the fact that the newest member of our creative department had risen to the challenge.

George never looked back. God bless Ivan Horvath.

(This next story was relayed to a handful of stunned creatives by an excited fellow copywriter I worked with early in my career. I'll never forget this interview story. You may want to remember it, too.)

An Indispensable Interviewing Tip

Rob returned to Dailey & Associates looking like he'd just won the California Lottery. "I got the job!!!" None of us could believe his good fortune. Rob had gotten hired by Chiat/Day. The best agency in town. One of the best in the entire country. The place every creative in town wanted to work at.

But the most amazing part wasn't that he got the job. It was how he got it.

"So I was sitting in Dave Butler's office and he was halfway through my portfolio. He was being nice, but he seemed far from blown away. I knew I had to do something."

Rob interrupted Dave. "Mr. Butler, I'd like to share something with you."

Butler stopped and looked up. "Okay, Rob."

Rob laid it on the line. "I just wanted to let you know that from the day I went into this business, I've dreamt of working for Chiat/Day... and, I wanted you to know that if you were to hire me, I'd never give you a reason to regret it."

David Butler zipped Rob's portfolio shut without looking at another piece. "You have no idea how rarely I hear that, Rob. Can you start in two weeks?"

Rob appealed to David Butler on a far deeper level than his portfolio ever could. He made Dave a promise that compelled his new boss to invest in him. Rob sold himself that day. He spent almost a decade never letting David Butler regret the decision, and building an enviable portfolio in the process.

The moral of this story? Sometimes who you present is every bit as important as what you present.

Know a Good Assassin

In polite society, murder is universally frowned upon. Unfortunately, it's also frowned upon in advertising. So, what can you do when someone tries to tromp all over your game? Take the legal route. Literally. Develop a relationship with a good lawyer. You may never have to call on their skill set, but it's better to have them and not need them than vice versa.

For those reasons and more, I've found it's valuable to have a lawyer on your contact list. They don't come cheap. But, they are good to have access to when you get into higher-level jobs where promises are only as good as the paper they're drafted on.

You may be offered incentives beyond your yearly salary, like an ownership stake, equity in the agency, or bonuses based on achieving financial or creative milestones. Get that shit in writing, and have your lawyer look at everything. Promises don't mean much unless you've got a legally binding agreement.

Getting stuff notarized is like money in the bank. Keep all your paperwork in a safe place, like a safe deposit box, as opposed to your desk drawer at the office where you squirrel away your Triscuits and supply of three-ply toilet paper.

And please heed my advice about murder. That's better left to those Netflix dramas you've been binge-watching.

Ask and Ye Might Receive

Every interaction you have with another human being is a form of negotiation. Some negotiations are rather low on the importance scale, like when you want to go out and party while your significant other wants to chill at home.

But in other cases, it could mean the difference between being miserable or getting what you deserve. Therefore, it stands to reason that you should get good at the art of negotiation.

The first step is to study your hand with brutal honesty. Just wanting something isn't enough. If you feel you deserve something, be prepared to make your case why. If you don't present your case with confidence and clarity, you're not likely to convince the powers that be to loosen the purse strings and/or promote you.

Another factor to consider is timing. If you're looking for a raise, don't ask after you've just come back from a vacation. Let your suntan fade, or wait until you're coming off a strong effort on a big project. Strike when your worth is impossible to ignore.

Remember that money isn't everything when negotiating. If you can't get what you want in dollars, ask for more vacation time or flex days that allow you the freedom to work where and when you please. Or, ask your employer to sponsor your attendance at conferences or training seminars that expand your skill set. Look for ways that increase your value to your agency.

Get all agreements in writing.

After years of sharpening my negotiating skills, I either get what I want from the get-go, or I politely pass. You should do the same.

Cover your Ass. Seriously

One of the things you'll notice about most Human Resources people is that they have serious control issues. They hold the keys to the castle and know all the dirty little secrets in the office. It's their job to control the chaos. If this sounds like someone you don't want to piss off, you're right.

HR can mess with you in a lot of ways, none of them pleasant. They don't like being challenged, and they have the ears of the most important players at the agency. They know how much everyone makes, and can easily kibosh your raise or promotion.

They have the messiest jobs in the world, as far as I'm concerned. Making their jobs just a little easier is a smart way to play your hand. Don't give them a reason to hunt you down for a private conversation.

Case in point. Years ago when I was young, and dumb, and didn't understand what human resource people do, I got an impromptu visit from the HR manager at Ketchum Advertising. She'd received a complaint that I had bared my ass in the office. The context of the situation was beside the point, and not open for debate. I did it, and she'd heard about it. It was completely unacceptable. Seeing it typed out on paper was a real eye-opener.

I'd been graphically lewd in what I considered the privacy of my office, and directed my actions towards a fellow creative. Unfortunately, somebody else whom it wasn't directed at caught wind of it, no pun intended. I had no choice but to sign a piece of paper that went into my permanent personnel file. That day would be my only warning. If anything like that ever happened again, I was toast.

I'd never felt like more of a dipshit in my entire adult life. There I was, a father, a husband, and a so-called professional treating the creative department as if it was a frat house. I was lucky I didn't get fired on the spot. These days, I likely would have been.

Please, don't ever make the mistake of thinking you're immune from getting your ass handed to you. My personnel file from Ketchum probably exists to this day in the cloud somewhere. I only hope some poor intern didn't have to re-input my offense for the digital age.

The moral here? Everyone draws the line differently on what is and isn't proper behavior in the workplace. An agency is not your tree fort. Your colleagues are not your frat brothers. Don't aspire to be Adland's village idiot.

There are enough village idiots in advertising already.

Squeezing One Out for the Team

Sometimes building client trust can be as simple as taking one for the team. Or letting one go. My old partner, Richard Kile, from my L.A. advertising days, reminded me of this great moment in the annals of client relations.

One day, we were on a TV shoot with the director of marketing for Clothestime, a discount women's fashion account. Lisa was a very cool client with a nice sense of style, who put up with having Richard Kile and me as her creative team for two full years.

The commercial's director came over to the video playback monitor. We all hovered closely around the small screen reviewing the last scene to make sure we were happy with what he'd just shot. Shifting forward towards the monitor, Lisa accidentally farted, and loudly. The director, his production people, and the agency team all stopped in their tracks. It was a truly awkward moment.

Lisa was mortified.

Seeing an opportunity to assist a client in need, I took a deep breath and pressed out a loud fart of my own. The entire crew burst into laughter.

Later that day, Lisa thanked me for my heroic act in front of Richard Kile. "You don't have to thank him, Lisa," my partner said. "He does that for me at least three times a day." True.

The moral of the story? Sometimes raising a minor stink is the best thing you can do for the sake of client relations.

The Vast Importance of Impulse Control

For some reason, Della Femina had more than its share of characters in the late '80s and early '90s. You had Dick Sittig, who launched out of there like a rocket. Jackie Sisson, who perfected the art of being an acidic cynic. Rick Carpenter, who looked like he was sent over from Mad Men central casting.

At the other end of the spectrum was an odd little fellow I'll call "Cal". He was a paste-up guy in the print production bullpen but desperately wanted to be a copywriter. Even though he looked a bit like a discount Ralph Macchio, he was a nice kid, and his wide-eyed passion was hard to ignore.

A few creatives and I took him under our wings and tried to bring him along. It was a social experiment at best. Given Cal's determination and scrappy appeal, our collective efforts landed Cal a shot as a junior writer.

His work was coming along nicely, and his fledgling client skills were improving. One day, he was invited to come along to a presentation to our client, Isuzu. While Cal had been on the team that did the work, none of his ads had made the cut. He was mostly there for the sake of seasoning, and to get a feel for the presentation side of things.

The presentation was a bust.

The client, less than impressed, asked if there was any other work to show. Just as the creative director was delivering the tried-and-true "We'll go back to the agency and redouble our efforts" speech, Cal raised his hand like a student requesting a bathroom break.

The client looked Cal's way with curiosity, while the rest of us watched in what was soon to be utter disbelief.

"There was one campaign we didn't bring", said Cal. He went on to describe one of his ideas in great detail. In no time, the client realized why it wasn't in the batch presented, thanked Cal, and brought the meeting to a close.

As soon as we hit the parking lot, the CD pulled Cal aside and laid into him. Although they'd stepped several feet away from the rest of the group, we could hear it all.

It was explained to Cal in no uncertain terms that this could never happen again. Back at the agency, he was cornered by many ranking players as word spread of his astonishing fuck-up. He heard the riot act from one and all – including Human Resources, who impressed upon him that he was officially on their "watch list."

Needless to say, Cal didn't attend any more client presentations for quite some time. He was given the worst assignments as punishment but performed them without complaint. To his credit, he did everything possible to show that he had learned his lesson, and slowly rebuilt his credibility.

Cal was living proof that you can come back from anything if you handle your mistakes right.

A year or so later, a more mature Cal finally made it back to a presentation for another client. His attitude was all positivity. Again, the presentation was less than successful, and the client asked a similar question to the one asked by our largest client so many months before. Everyone held their breath for a second, fearing the worst.

Cal didn't utter so much as a peep. The relief among us all was palpable. The creative director reached across the table to shake the client's hand. Everyone stood and started gathering their things. That's when Cal chimed in.

"Well, there was one other idea ..."

How to Avoid Becoming Fossil Fuel

During a time I was running a global agency's Denver office, the network's CEO was a brilliant older gentleman who couldn't have impressed me more. David had been elected into the Advertising Hall of Fame in 2007. What makes the accomplishment even more extraordinary was that he was inducted as an account guy.

Before he'd joined the upper ranks of our agency, he had been the CEO of Interpublic, which is about as big a job as any in advertising.

When he was aged-out of the Interpublic gig, he did something you might not expect a retired advertising legend to do. He asked a Silicon Valley tech startup for an internship.

Google gave him one.

During his internship, David, by then in his late sixties, educated himself about digital and social. He soaked it up like a sponge. He soon leveraged his learning into another CEO gig at my new global agency.

Most guys retire when they reach the top and get their gold watch. Not this dude. David circled back to the bottom of the food chain. He relearned enough to make himself dangerous all over again. I'll be the first to tell you that ageism runs rampant in advertising. But some people just refuse to be stopped.

My agency was damn lucky to have David at the top.

I took the liberty of sharing this story so far without mentioning David's last name. It's Bell. You can find him in the Advertising Hall of Fame. Maybe he'll be inducted twice. Once as a renowned account person, and again as the world's smartest intern.

Ted, the Swizzle Stick of Fate

Long before there was a successful series of tech talks known as TED, there was a modified cocktail swizzle stick of the same name that held amazing powers of production prowess.

This Ted belonged to an executive producer I worked with at BBDO. I loved the guy. His name was Joe Knisley, and he carried a shortened cocktail swizzle stick with a 90-degree bend melted into it. He affectionately called his plastic compadre "Ted".

Ted was never far from Joe's grasp. Joe would whip Ted out whenever situations got thick, hold it close to his mouth, and seek Ted's all-knowing wisdom.

"The director's bid is too high, Ted. I think we're screwed. What do we do now?" He'd then shift his beloved Ted to one ear and listen intently as Ted whispered the worldly advice of a repurposed swizzle stick. "Good idea, man. I hadn't thought of that."

Everybody who chooses advertising as a career path needs a Ted. My father was mine until he passed away in 2010.

I hope this book will be yours.

DEDICATION & ACKNOWLEDGEMENTS

This survival guide is dedicated to a dead Guy.

Dad would have appreciated the irony.

My father, Guy Day, was my career counselor, mentor, and ethical advertising compass for over twenty years until his death in 2010. But while he was my single biggest influence from a career standpoint, he was not alone in guiding me.

A lot of people deserve my heartfelt thanks.

I'll start with my beautiful and whip-smart wife, Debbie, who keeps me on my toes, well-fed, and feeling rather fortunate to have the life we do. She is the most selfless person I've ever met. Thanks for letting me and our boys be your working projects.

Which brings me to Cameron and Drew, and my extended family, who graciously put up with me through thick and thin, and ushered me into adulthood. My mother, Annette; my sister, Colleen, who had the good sense to steer clear of advertising; and last but not least, my brother, Bill, who did not.

I've always considered my brother Bill to be the most talented writer in my family, although our firstborn may give him a run for his money.

Bill brought a ton of wit and wisdom to this book as an editor and collaborator riding shotgun alongside me for every page of this journey, polishing and tumbling every word until it rose to a level that would've made our pop proud.

This shout-out doesn't come close to properly covering Bill's contributions. My son, Cameron, also took a read through this as did Tom Schmidt, a proofreader and fellow copywriter, and both contributed nicely to what I hoped was the final draft. [It wasn't.]

Another key person is Jean Craig, who hired me twice, and taught me more than I ever realized at the time. Jean graciously agreed to put fresh eyes on the first draft of this book. Her mentorship and continued support cannot be expressed in mere words, try as I might. I loved working for you, Jean.

A small handful of folks read drafts of my book and helped smooth out the bumps. Ari Echt, Justin Oberman, Todd Nolley, Matt Stiker, Luke Sullivan, Rick Boyko, Rachel Edwards, Mia Nogueira, Fred S. Goldberg, Chuck Guest, Jeff Gelberg, Jay Roth, Greg Harrison, Nikhil "eagle eye" Rajagopalan and finally Chase Zreet, who inspired me to write this book after reading my Diesel pitch story a few years ago.

To the handful of advertising book authors who also generously offered me advice about publishing a niche book. Thomas Kemeny, Howie Cohen, Fred S. Goldberg, Luke Sullivan, Bruce Bendinger, Laurence Minsky, and Mat Zucker all provided invaluable counsel.

To my earliest bosses, many of whom believed in me before I believed in myself. Mel Newhoff, Ivan Horvath, Ron Goodwin, Rick Carpenter, Jackie Sisson, Richie Russo, and, of course, Jean.

To my partners in crime, who gave me more laughs and good material than any writer could hope for. Margie Sillman, Todd McVey, David Heise, Ron Goodwyn, Barbara "Tortellini" Travis, Mike Pitzer, Patrick Aroff, Richie Kile, Kevin McCarthy, April Thomas, Bill Northrup, Walt Harris, Greg Harrison, David Crawford, Lou Flores, James Mikus, Rob Lewis, Larry Leung, Larry Jarvis, Matt Mowatt, Guy Kirkland, Dave Ayriss, and finally Clark Evans, who graciously confided in me that Lee Clow is not a fan of colored type. We changed his kind words in the foreword accordingly. **Whew.**

To the friends and colleagues from all disciplines, in and out of advertising, who have proven instrumental in my world. Steve Batchelor, Eric Coolbaugh, Clay Langdon, Michael Anderson, "Gentleman Joe" Knisely, Gary Wise, Kevin Peake, Morgan Rowe, Adam Nelson, Ricky Lambert, and Michael "hang-the-quotation-marks-on-the-back-cover" Thomas.

I miss being around you people, particularly when good ideas are eluding me.

I'd also like to acknowledge a few higher-ups who bet on me as a writer, a creative director, or both. Christoph Becker and Bryan Thomas, Mark McGarrah and Bryan Jessee, Steve, Roy, Judy & Tim, Bob Kresser and Jean Craig, Bill Morden and the Colonel, Cliff "I come from funny" Einstein, Bill Schumacher, Joe McDonagh, Benoit and Robin.

To my freelance clients, who've made it possible for me to carve out a living by writing more than I shower: Kyle, Josh, Chris, Prentice, Eric, Doug, Brad, Craig, Mark, Bryan, James, Mars, Courtney, Eric and Carolyn, Chuck and Billy, Will, and those who booked me solo or have given assignments to Two-Headed Cam, muchos gracias.

To my freelance partners, who put up with my penchant for early mornings, mantra writing ways and Google Drive docs that often resemble a crime scene, especially Guy Kirkland and David Ayriss, and my son Cameron, with whom I've recently starting Two-headed Cam, a story better revealed on my website.

I'd be remiss if I didn't thank the fine folks who read *CYWMO* and provided a blurb for my book's back cover or quotes pages: Terry Balagia, Toby Barlow, Andrew Boulton, Bryan Carter, Will Chau, Rick Boyko, Fred S. Goldberg, Jeff Graham, Shayna Levin Brown, Kenneth L. Marcus, Ernie Schenck, Luke Sullivan, and Vikki Ross.

And finally, those who inadvertently taught me what not to do when I rose to their level, I don't imagine you'll waste a moment of your precious time reading this.

If history is any indication, I'll live.

ABOUT MY WORK:

I made the decision to leave my actual work out of this book but not because it sucks. IMO, at least. You can see much of the stuff I've written about on my website. Visit: iamcameronday.com

ABOUT MY BOOK'S DESIGN:

UK-based graphic designer, Andrew Mark Lawrence brought this survival guide style and substance well beyond my words. Andrew is truly remarkable and I'm lucky he said yes. Visit: graphicdesignfutures.com

ABOUT THE COVER:

Beau Hanson thought of the cover idea. He's a great human being and art director. His equally great friends, husband-and-wife team, The Voorhes, created the "gum-brain" prop and photo. Visit: thevoorhes.com

ABOUT THE ARCHIVAL IMAGES:

I reached out to Charles Spencer Anderson about using images from his archives. He was a real pleasure to work with. I highly recommend him, and his amazing library. Thank you, Charles. Visit: CSAimages.com

ABOUT STICKY INTELLECT:

In creating my own publishing imprint for the "CWYMO" trilogy, I needed a logo. I reached for the stars and Austin-based designer, Robert Lin, made the magic happen. He's super awesome. And super talented. Visit: robertlindesign.com

ABOUT THE ADVERTISING SURVIVAL GUIDE TRILOGY:

All books in the Advertising Survival Guide trilogy are available through Amazon Books in both print and Kindle editions. Hand-signed editions are available from the author via his personal advertising website. That is all. Thank you. Visit: www.iamcameronday.com

Made in the USA
Columbia, SC
24 October 2024

44576215R00120